Loose WOMEN
LET LOOSE!

Loose WOMEN
LET LOOSE!

hamlyn

OUR LIFE LESSONS REVEALED

An Hachette UK Company
www.hachette.co.uk

First published in Great Britain in 2019 by Hamlyn, an imprint of
Octopus Publishing Group Ltd
Carmelite House
50 Victoria Embankment
London EC4Y 0DZ
www.octopusbooks.co.uk

ISBN 978-0-600-63635-9

A CIP catalogue record for this book is available from the British Library.

Printed and bound in UK

10 9 8 7 6 5 4 3 2 1

General Editor and Writer: Christian Guiltenane

Publishing Director: Trevor Davies
Art Director: Yasia Williams-Leedham
Senior Editor: Louise McKeever
Production Controller: Grace O'Byrne

Cover photographer: Mark Harrison
Designer: Siaron Hughes
Illustrator: Frank Ramspott at iStockphoto.com
Copy-editor: Liz Marvin

Picture credits:
Page iv, below – Ken McKay/ITV/Shutterstock
Page vi, above – ITV/Shutterstock
Page xvi – Steve Meddle/ITV/Shutterstock
Images reproduced with the permission of ITV and the Loose Women.

The advice in this book is believed to be correct at the time of printing, but the
authors and the publishers accept no liability for actions inspired by this book.

—❤—

CONTENTS

INTRODUCTION

Hello ladies, how are you? Are you having a good week? Well it's about to get a lot better now that you've got this wonderful book in your hands.

If like many of us you are feeling lost, confused, sad, directionless or tired and are in need of a pick-me-up and a laugh, then you've come to the right place. Welcome to our brand-new *Loose Women* book, packed with funny, heart-warming and touching stories that we hope will enlighten and entertain you in equal measure.

For more than twenty years we have been sharing very personal stories about our lives with you, our ever-devoted and loyal extended family, so you'll know what to expect. And as we all know, it's good to share. Not only to get things off our chests once and for all but also to let other women know that they are not alone in all the things that they go through in day-to-day life.

And we're so pleased to hear that our stories mean so much to you. The number of messages we receive from all of you telling us that you identify with the ups-and-downs that we go through is truly phenomenal.

Sometimes we don't take a moment to stop and think about the things that have happened to us and the lessons that we have learned along the way. But this book does that. Within these pages we will share our very honest truths about love and heartache, friendships and fallouts, motherhood and loss, and lots more besides.

Consider this a book that will help you to navigate life when it needs direction and bring some light into your day. We won't tell you how to live your life of course, only you can do that, but perhaps reading our stories will make you stop and think, and teach you a little life lesson or two.

Come and join the conversation.

Coleen, Nadia, Jane, Janet, Gloria, Saira, Kaye

PART 1
LOVE AND RELATIONSHIPS

From an early age, most of us have spent many a waking day wondering if and when Mr Right will finally walk into our lives, whisk us off our feet and dash us up the aisle so that we can live happily ever after.

As you know, most of our savvy Loose Ladies are believers in love. Jane Moore says that 'love is when you get to know somebody and all of their faults – and you love them in spite of that', while Coleen Nolan declares that, as she is 'in love with love', she has cherished every one of her partners 'for different reasons and in different ways'.

Even Janet Street-Porter once uncharacteristically surmised that 'love is when you see someone and you feel physically ill if you are not in contact with them'.

The course of true love isn't always easy and our Loose Women are testament to that! Between the seven of them featured in this book, they have notched up eleven marriages and seven divorces – four of them Janet's! They've been there, done it, bought the T-shirt and are now sharing their wisdom in these pages.

Finding love, holding on to it or trying to make what we already have even better not only takes up a significant amount of time but also proves to be a series of exhausting challenges, whether you're single or in that much sought after-relationship.

Love can be a difficult concept to navigate successfully, but it's one we've all grown up to believe is our ultimate destiny, thanks to all those cutesy Disney flicks and heart-tugging romcoms. As a result, we have all embarked on our life path not only to carve out a successful career but, more importantly, to find that special someone to share it with too.

If you want to find yourself a beau, you need to get out there smartish and find one in whichever way you feel fit. If you're having problems with your other half, then you *must* take the bull by the horns and sort the problem out. For every woman, there is a different journey with different solutions. No two experiences are the same, as our Loose Women have proved over and over again.

In this section, our Loose Ladies open up about what they have learned about falling in love, getting married, dealing with hardships, having affairs and deciding to pull the plug on their relationships. So put the kettle on, sit back in your favourite spot and be inspired...

EARLY DAYS

FINDING THE ONE

Remember that episode of *Friends* where Phoebe explained to lovelorn Ross that on–off girlfriend Rachel was his lobster? According to the 'Smelly Cat' songstress, 'it is a known fact that lobsters fall in love and mate for life'. While this is not strictly true, the phrase has still become synonymous with the concept of The One – that idea that there is someone out there who we are meant to be with forever, who it is our destiny to meet.

Perhaps you've already found them or maybe you think it's a load of old codswallop. One thing's for sure though, if you're currently single and you're interested in a relationship, the only way to find out if that perfect man is out there is to go and have a look!

If we can learn to play it right, the dating scene can be a lot of fun. That dating app you've just rolled your eyes at? Keep scrolling and maybe there's someone special just waiting to hear from you. That night out you're about to say no to? Perhaps that's when you'll find a handsome stranger standing at the bar. Whether you're a cynic or a romantic at heart; whether you believe there is one special person for everyone or not, there's no harm in having a look, is there?!

So what do our Loose Women think about trying to find The One?

Coleen Nolan says that although there once was a time during her younger years when she'd believed in finding that one special someone, her roller-coaster life experience has made it quite clear that potentially there was – and still could be – *more* than one Mr Right to seek out.

'When I was younger, I definitely believed in The One,' she says. 'Still to this day, I watch all the romantic films and read romantic novels. But now I believe there is "The One for *now*".'

The One for now? An interesting concept and a much more sensible and realistic way of looking at relationships. Right? From what we see around the *Loose Women* table, many of us are likely to enter into two or three relationships throughout our lifetime. During each of these relationships, we feel committed and totally and utterly convinced that we will be with those other halves until the end of time. However, due to unforeseen circumstances or utter foolishness on the part of one half of the couple, a once thriving union can be brought suddenly and painfully to a sad end, a scenario that Gloria Hunniford is only too familiar with.

'I got married at 21, and he was my forever one,' she says of her first husband, Don Keating, whom she divorced in 1992 after ten years of marriage. 'We were going to have children and be together forever. But in life, things happen. And now, my second husband, Stephen, is The One. And we have just celebrated our twentieth anniversary.'

Jane Moore thinks that spending lots of time chasing after this elusive, perfect man is only setting ourselves up for disappointment. She says she has been keen to instil in her daughters, Ellie, Grace and Lauren, that it's not necessarily worth waiting for the picture-perfect Prince Charming whom so many conjure up in their minds.

'As a concept, The One is a nice idea, but when you think about the reality – what are the chances you'll meet that "One"? Does that mean if you don't, you spend your entire life on your own?' Instead, she says, 'Love is a decision and not just a feeling. If your state of mind is that it's forever, and your partner has the same state of mind, chances are you'll survive the course.'

When she was a junior reporter, Jane interviewed couples celebrating their golden-wedding anniversary and asked them about the secret to the longevity of their relationships. 'I remember asking one of the couples if her husband was her perfect man, and she said, "He has all his own teeth!" That was her only requirement!' Jane says.

'I wouldn't tell my daughters there's no "One",' Jane affirms. 'But if I saw them with someone kind and lovely who they thought wasn't good-looking or tall enough, and just wasn't The One, I'd tell them not to throw him away, because of all his other lovely qualities.'

Gloria says her experience of seeking out potential husbands was different growing up in rural Northern Ireland because she had to live up to certain expectations. 'I was of the era where if you weren't engaged to be married by the time you were 19 or 20, you were regarded as being on the shelf,' she comments. 'It was expected that you would get married. I still think that in rural areas, family values are often different from those in cities.'

However, Saira Khan reckons that we have been conditioned to believe that we are supposed to seek out just one person for life, when in fact we may need to find various suitors throughout our lives who will provide us with different forms of support. 'I think we are brainwashed into thinking there is just The One,' Saira says. 'It's the Hollywood dream, that magical moment where you meet The One, have kids and live happily ever after. But I don't believe in this. I don't think there is just one person. I think there are various people who could potentially come into our lives at different points.'

She explains that when we're younger, we tend to need people who will encourage us to have fun, which is what she did, in spite of her strict religious upbringing. When you are ready to settle with kids, you are looking for someone who will be a good father and will be kind. Then, after having kids, we may go on a big journey that may require someone new. 'I have said to my husband, "I don't think there is one person to fulfil all our needs",' she says.

While she says that she and her husband Steve – who she has been with for almost 15 years – are happy, and she feels fulfilled, she is aware that dynamics could change over time.

'You grow as a person. You're not the same person at 50 that you were at 20 and your partner won't be the same person after many years, especially after kids,' she muses. 'We all change. We just put up and shut up, and I think that leads to a lot of unhappiness. I think we need to talk about different avenues.'

Saira says that because she and her husband come from a business background they tend to look at relationship issues in the same way they would a business one. 'I am never scared about discussing our relationship,' she says. 'In any marriage there are ups-and-downs. But Steve and I are used to talking about problems and finding solutions. We have had some very serious chats during our marriage, like, "Are we doing the right thing?", "Are we happy?" and we have confronted issues head on. And that's why we are still together. We iron out a lot of the problems as we go.'

IS THERE SUCH A THING AS LOVE AT FIRST SIGHT?

Do you believe that a person can fall in love with someone after just one meeting? Or do you mistake an instant personality connection for more? Some say that to truly fall in love we need to get to know someone over years before a deep love can be formed.

Nadia Sawalha learnt first hand that love at first sight does exist, having experienced it when she met TV director Mark on the set of TV dating show – *Perfect Partner* – in 2002. There was a spark between them from day one. She says, 'Really quickly the relationship became very intense. Although there were many differences between us – we just had this incredible chemistry.'

Nadia admits that she was even surprised at herself with how quickly the relationship developed, 'All I can say is – when you know, you know.'

A baby and marriage followed very soon after, which Nadia truly believes strengthened their commitment to making the relationship work long-term.

When Nadia now reflects back on the time she says that 'It was an exciting whirlwind that nobody believed would last the course of time. But here we both are – 17 years later. Through a lot of hard work, commitment and loyalty we're still together... And we take one day at a time.'

Coleen agrees that 'you can walk away from someone and think you already have that connection, and say to yourself, "I can't wait to see them again".'

Jane isn't so sure: 'I don't believe you can have love at first sight. Lust perhaps, but not love.'

Janet remembers a time she was set up on a blind date by a work colleague, during which she experienced anything but *love* at first sight...

'A girl I worked with had met a man in a bar who was obsessed with me and told him, "I can introduce you to Janet." He asked, "Can I have lunch with her?" and she told him, "I'll introduce you to Janet if you agree to go out with me afterwards." As my boyfriend was away on tour, I agreed to meet him. I picked a restaurant miles from anywhere that had flattering dim lighting. When I arrived I could see this really fit bloke sitting in a candlelit alcove. I sat down and I said, "I'm only here because of the deal you made." And he said, "Well let's just enjoy it, shall we?" That was at 1.30pm. By 4pm I was back his place and we then went on to have an affair for four or five months.'

As we all know, Janet is a woman who enjoys the sexual side of relationships and enthusiastically encourages people to have sex as early as possible. 'Have sex on the first or second date,' she declares. 'If you have sex with them and you are not compatible you might as well dump them straight away. I think sometimes there are occasions when you can tell if there is potential for improvement and if so then you can take it further. But if they're bad in bed, there's no point in going back.'

But as we know, many relationships build over time, and someone you have known for some time suddenly becomes someone you fall madly in love with.

Gloria says that she thinks the strongest relationships are based on more than physical looks and instant connections. 'When we're young, all we're thinking about is, "What does he look like, what does he drive, where's he going to take me, where's he going to take me for dinner?" It's all about looks and sex I suppose. Whereas, as you get older, particularly when you move on to a second marriage, you look for totally different things. I got married at 21 and my husband was marvellous. But I think with a second marriage you are looking for different attributes.

'By the time I met Stephen, I already had my children; Caron, my daughter, was about to have a baby, I already had a roof over my head and I had a good job, so I was interested in meeting somebody to go to the theatre with, go out for dinner, do things with. But I wasn't particularly looking for marriage and a long-term thing.

'Stephen and I went out with each other for a year before anything happened. I fancied him like mad and he used to say to me, "When are we going to get this together?" But I just wasn't in the right space at that time. So I'd say, "Look, when the time is right". But what I learned during that year was that we liked each other, we could talk about anything – and we still talk about everything and anything.'

Kaye Adams agrees that sometimes finding true love takes time and that it's not always wise to rush into a relationship. "When I met my partner Ian I didn't really think he was my type,' she recalls of her relationship, which has spanned over 30 years. 'I was probably looking for a conventionally handsome, suited-and-booted professional guy. And I look back on that with a slight sense of embarrassment. I met Ian through mutual friends. He dressed like a complete beatnik. He had wild Brian May style hair, his favourite coat was an East German army surplus coat that he got from some flea market in Italy. So he was about as opposite to what I thought I wanted as you could possibly get. He was a kind of tennis coach who wandered the world. I would say we got on enough, but I did not think of him romantically one iota, I have to say, not one iota.'

So far from love at first sight, Kaye explains that their bond grew over time until, one night at dinner, it dawned on the pair that stronger feelings than friendship gripped them. 'Then we went out one night for a pizza and that was it – everything just clicked into place. But it had been a real slow burner. Although we had known each other for a while, he travelled a lot so I never once thought of him romantically. For one, I thought that he was actually very full of himself, which, it turned out, is the opposite of the truth! He was also very slim and fit; he had long, slim legs and I thought, I can't go out with a man who's skinnier than me! He's going to make me feel fat! But then, after that night, everything just clicked into place, and we fell in love!'

CAN AGE-GAP RELATIONSHIPS WORK?

Why is it that when older guys date younger women nobody seems to bat an eyelid, yet if a woman has the audacity to be seen with a man a few years her junior all hell breaks loose?

Isn't dating all about a meeting of minds and bodies regardless of the year you were born? Or is it? Can couples with decades between them make it work or are age-gap relationships always destined for disaster, no matter how much society's expectations change?

Nadia, who is seven years older than her husband Mark, says that when she was younger, she was definitely guilty of being judgemental about age-gap relationships.

'But now I have many friends who are in wonderful age-gap relationships, including my fabulous friends Carol McGiffin and Denise Welch. However, having said that, if I'm really honest, if one of my daughters had a relationship with a man twice her age I would have real concerns. Though it's probably a terrible thing to say – I would try and influence her decision, maybe even resorting to underhand tactics!' she laughs.

Coleen agrees that she's at a time in her life when she knows that going out with a younger guy just wouldn't work for her. 'I have a rule that I couldn't date somebody I could have given birth to!' she chuckles. 'Don't get me wrong, there's nothing wrong in looking. I like to look. But no, it would make me feel older, and I know they would do things and I would think, "Oh God, grow up!" Besides, if I dated a younger guy, I wouldn't know whether to make them a cup of tea or breastfeed them!'

Saira says that although in principle she is OK with an age gap, she does think it will cause problems in the long-run. 'I'm a pretty open-minded person about this, but I do think happiness can't last for long,' she reflects. 'I mean, at the beginning it will be fantastic, but then as the couple get older, the older of the two might slow down and lethargy will set in – as I have experienced myself – while the younger person might get bored and perhaps even resentful.'

Saira admits that she finds a relationship where the man is much older harder to accept. 'When I see men with younger women I have a problem,' she confesses. 'I'm not sure if it's because I've been conditioned to think that. But when I see an older woman with a younger guy, it feels like the younger man must know what he wants. In my head, if he goes for an older lady, it means that he's seeking intelligence, confidence and wisdom, and is looking for more than a physical relationship. While with older men, I can't help but feel he's just after a younger model and not much else.'

Jane isn't sure when it comes to age-gap relationships. 'It all depends when it is in your life,' she explains. 'I mean, look at someone like Kylie Minogue [who dated Joshua Sasse, an actor almost half her age] – she looks amazing! Anyone would want to date her. But if you face the 20-year age gap when you're 16 and they're 36, or the other way round even, that would seem sort of odd. So I guess it kind of depends where you are.'

Jane confesses that in her forties and fifties, she has regularly caught the eye of younger men but has never been sure what to make of it. 'I have been approached, but I look past them and wonder where's the friend that's put them up to this. I've always got that in the back of my mind.'

Kaye says she has seen age-gap relationships work within her circle, citing Carol McGiffin and her husband Mark, who is around 18 years younger than the *Loose Women* panellist. However, she does admit that she was sceptical about their future. 'I remember exactly when she started going out with Mark,' Kaye says. "She met him at a party, a Christmas party, and then we were at a book launch a few months later, and I do remember at the time thinking that they will never last because there was such an age difference. But I was wrong, and they have lasted.'

However, Kaye admits that if she saw a relationship between a man in his twilight years and a woman in her thirties, she would most definitely be curious about the nature of their relationship.

'I don't think suspicious is the word I'd use,' she says. 'But you always have questions about things that are outside of the norm, and there's no doubt that kind of age gap is well outside the norm. But that doesn't mean that it can't work or that it's wrong or that it's something born out of suspicious reasons. It's just doesn't happen very much and I guess it doesn't happen very much for a reason, because it's difficult, isn't it? It's all very well when there's somebody who's 25 and there's someone who is 45, and they're both still very much at the top of their game. When that becomes 45 and 65, or 55 and 75, life changes, circumstances change, so I think those relationships are under or can be under greater strain – but that doesn't mean that they can't work.'

Gloria says she is confident that age-gap couples are able to forge strong relationships but thinks that sometimes it's those looking on who have the biggest problem. 'I don't think you can generalise too much, because I think some of them work and some of them don't. I know a girl from the States who was with this man who was old enough to be her grandfather. I remember one time I was in a lift with them and she'd been for a swim in the pool and somebody said to him, "Make sure your granddaughter gets out of those wet clothes." It was quite awkward.'

Janet, unsurprisingly, thinks dating younger men can be a hoot. 'There's a lot to be said for toyboys, although I think that's demeaning as a phrase,' she says. 'It implies they're some kind of sex toy when in fact they have brains and have other uses as well.'

Janet explains that over the years she's 'had two boyfriends who were at least 20 years younger than me'. She recalls her time with TV presenter Normski with a warm, nostalgic smile. 'He was fantastic. Very clever and entertaining to be around and I enjoyed every minute of being with him.' She then adds, 'Until after five years when I couldn't listen to his music any more because it did my head in! So that was the end of our relationship, although we did stay friends.' Janet even wrote to his mother afterwards to say 'how much I adored her and I was sorry I was handing him back!'

However, the other experience Janet had with a younger guy proved to be an experience that left a rather nasty taste. 'When I was 49 I married someone in their twenties – that was my midlife crisis and I freely admit that.'

But Janet says she is proud of the fact that her age is just a meaningless number when it comes to going out with men. 'My third husband was 19 years older than me,' she recalls, 'and the most annoying thing was that the television was permanently on something green, whether it was rugby, football or cricket.'

DATING POSH MEN

If age-gap relationships are hard enough, how easy is it for us to embark on a romance with someone from a different social background? Well, it's worked for Meghan Markle and Prince Harry – they couldn't have come from more opposing backgrounds.

However, the unlikely marriage of East London rapper Professor Green and *Made in Chelsea* socialite and heir to the Quality Street empire Millie Mackintosh sadly lasted no longer than two years.

So can two people from very different backgrounds fall in love and live happily ever after?

Jane isn't entirely convinced that they can, having herself spent her younger days dating several posh guys, and feeling intimidated by their lifestyle. 'The boys were absolutely fine to me, but when I used to go back to their house it'd be this whacking great mansion in the countryside, while I used to live in a terraced house,' she recalls. 'It was more their parents I was intimidated by, as well as the lifestyle, with me thinking, "Oh my God, are they going to think I'm really common?" They probably did, because I'm not with them any more!'

While Jane acknowledges couples from different social backgrounds can get on, she fears the social divide could eventually cause a massive wedge in a flourishing relationship because couples might struggle in finding areas of commonality.

'My husband and I both came from a similar background, growing up on council estates, so we quite often have nostalgic conversations about our childhoods,' she explains. 'And I sometimes think that in a relationship where you come from very different places on the broad spectrum of life, maybe those arguments suddenly become, "Oh yeah, well you wouldn't understand that because you come from a wealthy family."'

Coleen is all for a bit of social integration, suggesting that these differences in background might actually be the reason a couple is attracted to each other in the first place. 'You're both so different,' she says. 'It's the type of person you've never been out with before.'

However, when it comes down to it, she says she simply couldn't go out with a hoity-toity aristocrat. 'If I was asked out by somebody really rich or really posh, I would feel like *My Fair Lady*. I'd have to have elocution lessons and learn how to eat properly and work out what fork I'd use. It's not them I'd be worried about, it's my own insecurities.'

Saira thinks that in principle these relationships can work, but worries that external pressures might cause issues later on. 'Couples can absolutely do it, but you need a lot of confidence to make it last,' she says.

'I come from a different cultural background to Steve, but socially and economically we have the same background so we are on level ground. But would I want to go out with a toff? I'm not sure. But that's because it's not what I am attracted to. That said, wealth and money doesn't intimidate me. And I feel, in those worlds, it is others who make people feel awkward – their families and their friendship groups.'

LOOSE LESSONS

- Finding Mr Right might not happen in an instant. Sometimes the special one could develop from a friendship and already be right under your nose.

- Age ain't nothing but a number. As long as there is a connection and respect for one another, you can enjoy a fruitful relationship.

- Your guy may be Prince Harry's cousin once removed, but love can still flourish if you make that special connection.

SEX

ARE YOU GETTING ENOUGH?

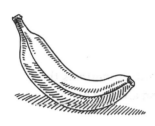

So... how often do you have sex? Once a week? Once a month? Er... once a year? Don't worry, you don't have to answer that out loud. But ask yourself – are you happy? Do you want more of it? Do you want less? Do you want it with other people? Or are you happy to do it on your own?

Nadia says, 'I think for most people in a long-term relationship with kids, dogs and goldfish to look after, it can sometimes be a challenge to find the time, space and peace to the get the same sex life that you did before the responsibilities piled up.'

Nadia chuckles and with a wink says, 'But where there's a will, there's a way.' She continues, 'It is important to make the time for one another... every so often! However tired, fat, miserable, exhausted or fed-up you feel, as far as I'm concerned, sex is an important part of any loving relationship. Having said that, I have a number of friends who no longer have sex, but are very happy. So, one size does not fit all. Over the last 20 years on *Loose Women* I've been involved in many conversations about sex and I think that we probably all worry about it more than we need to.'

Saira Khan says she understands this situation all too well and admits there was a time in her relationship when the idea of having sex with husband Steve put the fear of God in her.

'I had a busy life, I had two young kids, I was very lucky to have all that in my life, but there were times when I felt like I wasn't interested in sex, that I just didn't want to do it,' she acknowledges. 'Don't get me wrong, I love my husband, he is the most amazing man in the world and we've been married for over 12 years. I absolutely hadn't gone off him. We would still cuddle up and watch TV all the time, but when it came to sex, there were times I found myself making excuses like, "Oh, I'm really tired." I would notice that at six o'clock, as soon as he walked through the door, I was in a panic because I was worried he'd want sex and I wouldn't be in the right place for it. This happened quite regularly and I started to ask myself was this normal? And then I'd feel like I was the only one this was happening to – that everybody else had got the best sex life in the world; they were all doing it except me!'

Saira publicly spoke out about her feelings of frustration, saying, 'I got to that stage when I said to my husband, "Look I'm just not in that place, if you really want to, go with somebody else." I just wanted to make him happy.'

At the time, she said: 'I feel embarrassed that I am talking about my life like this, but I just feel like if it's something I can share, hopefully other women out there who feel the same way won't feel alone and that to feel that it's just part of life and not an abnormal thing.'

After her public admission, Steve assured Saira that he would never stray and admitted that he was heartbroken that she had even considered that he might entertain the possibility.

'Steve was amazing,' she says with emotion. 'He assured me that it was something he would never contemplate doing and that he felt troubled and heartbroken that I had got to such a low point that I felt the need to say something like that.'

After talking through their issues, Saira and Steve thankfully managed to work things out and get their relationship back on track. 'We have taken some time out to discuss our relationship and things are fine now,' she says happily. 'Speaking out was so empowering. So many thousands of women have been through the same thing.'

Coleen says she has had a similar experience. 'Saira is not the only one who has gone through this... I went through a period when my libido was lower because the kids were younger and I was exhausted. But now they are grown up, I am much better.'

Coleen is also an agony aunt for a newspaper and she's had hundreds of messages from people going through the same thing.

'The whole thing gets messier because the couple don't talk about what is actually going on. I get men writing to me, saying, "I've tried everything, but I just don't feel she fancies me any more." The poor fellas take it as a real dent to their pride.

'I think we're all guilty of this... We get married and have kids, then a few years go by and we get into that rut of not consciously making the effort. Sex is a big part of our lives and it's best to be honest and talk about our problems instead of our men going out doing it behind our backs.'

Gloria thinks the importance we place on sex – and our need for it – naturally dissipates over the years because priorities in our lives change. 'When you're young, all you care about is how good looking your boyfriend is, or if he drives a nice car and if you're having lots of sex,' she explains. 'But when you get older there are different priorities. With older couples you have illness and various things that crop up. You have to deal with those things – it's not all about sex. There's a lot going on in a relationship and sex is just one aspect.'

Kaye says no one should feel bad about not wanting to have sex from time to time, and agrees with her fellow Loose Women that circumstances within a person's life can impact on their sex drive.

'The term "sexless relationship" is talked about like it's code for bad or fail. But all long-term relationships go through ebbs and flows. There are lots of people who've been in long-term relationships who at certain points get worn down.' Kaye says there have been times in her own life when she's had, 'things going on – when the kids were really small or when my parents were ill, I felt all over the place, and I was just trying to keep all the plates spinning and so my mind just wasn't *there* – and then I just went into a bunker and tried to survive. It might not have been fair on [my husband] Ian, but I just didn't want it at that time. I was just getting on, worrying about stuff, worrying about the kids and worrying that we're doing things right. As a woman, I sometimes don't feel carefree and want to scream, "Hey let's run through the daffodils!" That said, I'm much more likely to enjoy a good sex life when I'm happy.'

Nadia says in response, 'Bizarrely, I actually agree with Kaye on this one... and that's a rare thing! It's very difficult to feel gorgeous and sexy when you're in the spinning plates stage.'

DO YOU WANT TO SPICE UP YOUR SEX LIFE?

So we all agree that sometimes a relationship can get a bit stale. This of course can then have an impact on your sex life too.

Nadia laughs as she says, 'In a longer-term relationship it can definitely be difficult to be spontaneously spontaneous!'.

'I have been known to book a surprise lunch and a hotel for an afternoon nudge, nudge, wink, wink.'

'It's little moments like this that can really make a difference. I remember once that when we were leaving a hotel to go home, Mark was reluctant to leave because he didn't want the hotel staff to think that we'd booked the room for an intimate afternoon. I said to him that I had already paid for the room so all we had to do was to walk out. Eventually he agreed and we started walking through reception – and then made a run for it and ran down the road, until we collapsed in a fit of giggles.'

Coleen says that there was a time in her life when she couldn't get enough action from her then-husband, Shane. 'When I was very young, I used to have sex wherever it took my fancy,' she admits. 'We even did it in an NCP car park in Birmingham! We had got there early for a concert and the car park was empty. Things, er, happened, but when it was over we suddenly realised that the car park had got full and we hadn't noticed because the windows had steamed up. When you are younger you just do it anywhere.'

Coleen says that although she understands that relationships will, over time, experience lulls, she thinks it is up to the couple to keep the fire burning. 'I think we get lazy,' she says. 'When you first meet someone, in those few months the kids are never a problem, you make the effort and you find the time for sex. Then we become complacent and we tell each other that we haven't got time, that there's no one to look after the kids. But it was fine for the first year so why shouldn't we be as daring now? It's because we get lazy. So spontaneity is so important in keeping passions alive in a relationship.'

But spontaneous sex can sometimes be rather hazardous. Janet recalls a time she ended up with a sex-related injury. 'Back in the 1980s, waterbeds were a thing,' she laughs. 'My bloke and I had been to a party; we staggered up to my fourth-floor flat and jumped on the waterbed. But once we got on it the bed was like a wave machine and I kept banging my head against the wall. After a while, I felt I was going to be violently sick so I clambered off the bed and crawled across the room and into the bathroom, but once I got to the toilet I ended banging my head on the toilet!'

WOULD YOU BE HAPPY TO SATISFY YOURSELF WITH A SEX TOY?

The best thing about sex is that it doesn't always have to involve somebody else. After all, who really knows you best, eh? Luckily, there are a multitude of wonderful little tools and devices on the market that can bring a smile back to our faces and give a bouncy spring to our step. But not everyone is a fan of these battery-operated friends, as our Loose Women reveal...

Nadia says that when she attended a sex-toy party with some girlfriends she was rather taken aback by some of the appliances on show. 'I was horrified,' she recollects. 'The girls' night was great –

I was just absolutely horrified that the toys looked so realistic. They had included all the bits – such as the plumbing on the outside – in bright pink. It was just too much! I'd rather it was less realistic.'

Jane admits to being rather squeamish when it comes to toys, even though she has a secret stash of them hidden deep inside her closet at home.

'On my hen night, many, many years ago, my friends bought all the paraphernalia including furry handcuffs and, alarmingly, a chrome version of a Rampant Rabbit,' she explains. 'It's still all in a bag shoved in the back of a wardrobe gathering dust! My biggest worry is that one day I will get run over and my grieving kids will be sorting out my wardrobe and come across that bag and think the worst of me! I'm going straight home now to throw it all out!'

Coleen admits that she has used a buzzing sex toy in her time, although the results weren't quite what she was looking for. 'Years ago, there was a, er, very rampant product on the market that was everywhere,' she says. 'My friend had got me one as a present – strange friend, right? – and I put it away, out of mind. Then this one night Ray and I had this blazing row, so in a rage, I thought to myself, "Well, I don't need you because I have my friend." So I grabbed my toy and stomped off to the spare room where I got friendly with it. I'm not joking, but no sooner had I turned it on than I fell fast asleep, as I'd had a couple of glasses of wine, which always makes me sleepy. A little while later the sound of buzzing wakes me up and I'm thinking, "What's that buzzing?" Looking back, it wasn't the best experience I had.'

Gloria recalls an experience when she was recording a TV show, which left her rather red faced. 'I was filming *Cash in the Attic* and was rooting around in the drawers looking for something to auction when I stumbled across a collection of sex toys. I didn't know what they were at the time and started waving them around at the crew! However, I soon learned what they were for. But I didn't auction them off.'

But that's not the only time one of Gloria's TV shows has featured love aids. 'Recently on my consumer programme *Rip Off Britain*, I was in a shopping centre and asking people about their purchases. One young girl had been to Ann Summers and when I pulled a long-shaped parcel out of her bag I said, "Is this what I think it is?" In a panic she replied, "For God's sake don't show it on TV. My granny watches this show all the time!"'

IS THE MODERN WORLD RUINING OUR KIDS' SEX LIVES?

As we've already discussed, some women steer clear of sex when they're exhausted by work and family life, and it can be the same when they enter the menopause. But, surprisingly, it turns out that waves of young people are also giving up on going out and getting jiggy! According to research in 2018, millennials – that's anyone born after the mid-eighties and up until about 2000 – prefer to watch the telly on their tablets.

Saira is sympathetic to young people and admits that she can understand why they are choosing to put sex on the back burner for a while, although she reckons it has more to do with trying to navigate themselves through the tough journey of life.

'I think young people are so busy working and trying to save money to get a deposit for a house that they just don't have time or the strength to get intimate,' she reasons. 'If you're both working and you don't have that free time or energy, how are you ever going to get it on? I think the modern world is not conducive to being intimate. I genuinely think that young people are working so hard.'

Janet agrees with Saira but adds that she thinks young people's increasingly unhealthy relationship with their phones in general has seriously affected the way they interact with each other.

'I think it's about people not wanting to let go of their phones. They take their phones everywhere with them,' she asserts. 'Also, the working day has extended because the working day doesn't end when you leave *where* you work – it goes on holiday with you, it goes where you go out to eat in the evening or when you go home or travelling... People are always on their phones and that is so draining. I really think that has affected relationships in a really big way. It's interesting that in surveys about people's attitudes to sex, the younger generation – definitely people under 30 – are just not that bothered, in a way that's completely different to when I grew up.'

Gloria says she thinks modern technology is turning our kids into zombies. 'The whole IT thing drives me nuts. And by choice I don't indulge in it. I have a computer. I can receive and print off my scripts and so on, but I always phone people back. I never send an email,' she says. 'Stephen and I have ten grandchildren between us, and when they are on their phones all the time, it just drives me insane. So now I ban phones when they come for dinner. Because I want to talk to them. I want to hear what's happening in their lives.'

Saira believes this change has come about because sex is no longer something that is taboo. 'When we grew up, "doing it" was a big thing, wasn't it? It was naughty and at some stage you had to be married before you could do it. Now, it's so in your face: it's on every drama, every billboard, it's in every music video and you think, "Oh, so what?"'

Janet, however, reckons a big change happened 'when women took their tops off in newspapers', sparking a sexual revolution of sorts, in which women began getting vocal about their intimate moments. 'Suddenly, they're in newspapers with their tops off and the next thing you know women are discussing what went on in their bedrooms and how often they had sex,' she says. 'From that, we began to feel inadequate.'

Saira thinks, in the wake of the #MeToo movement, younger guys are less inclined to be proactive in their pursuit of women. 'I bet some young men are petrified of even asking somebody to go out with them nowadays!' she sympathises. 'They think, "Am I intimidating them? Will they report me for that?", so you've got all of that anxiety that goes with it now!'

IS LOSING YOUR VIRGINITY STILL A BIG DEAL?

We all remember our first time. Perhaps it was an utterly life-changing moment, or maybe it was simply a case of, 'Oh, is that it?' And, for some, it's an experience they'd rather forget.

Janet admits her first time was something she merely wanted to 'tick off her list'. 'It wasn't romantic, it was just a transaction,' she recalls. 'It was about as exciting as getting a bus pass or a railcard. It's just something you've got to go through.'

She says that from the age of 15 she was determined to lose her virginity. 'I chose the bloke because he had a lot of leather jackets and was the best-looking bloke in this club I used to go to,' she says. 'So I took his phone number, rang him up, went over to his house on the bus on a Saturday afternoon, did the deed, got the bus back home! It was nice. But the first time there's a bit of a squidge and then it's over, isn't it? I mean, an orchestra didn't come out of the cupboard and suddenly play.'

In fact, Janet remembers it as an experience that was far from heavenly. 'The first time you do it, it can be quite painful, and you're also a bit anxious about what bit goes where. After a few times you get better at it. Practice doesn't make perfect, but it definitely becomes more enjoyable. But the first time, oh, get over it.'

She asks, 'Why should the first person you have sex with be a person with whom you're going to have a relationship subsequently? I do admit that my attitude to sex and things like this, particularly losing your virginity, is more masculine than feminine. But there are lots of women who think like me! I'm not one in a million!'

Coleen, in contrast, enthuses, 'Mine was fabulous. It really was. It's probably because I did grow up watching all those romantic movies. I was madly in love with the guy I was with at the time, and there weren't violins, but they were in my head, I could hear them. I'll always remember it with such fondness. The first time is the one you always remember, you never forget your first time, good or bad, and for me it's nice to look back and think it was fabulous. It was everything I wanted and hoped it would be. Sadly, we didn't stay together but never mind.'

Nadia says she doesn't want to romanticise that particular rite of passage for her children. 'I would never want to give them a romantic ideal of what losing your virginity could be, as I don't want them to be disappointed if it's all rather pedestrian! If you think about all of the stories that you've heard from your friends over the years about how they lost their virginity, very few of them would say it was a beautiful experience with hearts and flowers.'

LOOSE LESSONS

- There's lots going on in our lives – work, kids, the latest addictive TV show – so we might not want sex all the time. It's normal, but don't keep it to yourself. Open up to your partner.

- As Coleen so wisely states, 'Spontaneity is important in keeping passions alive in a relationship.' So be imaginative!

- Brighten up your sex life and have some fun. Whatever your version of excitement is!

TYING THE KNOT

POPPING THE QUESTION

Getting engaged can be one of the most romantic moments in our lives. We've all heard of stories where a besotted suitor slips to one knee in a public place and tells his beloved that he wants to spend the rest of his life with her. Then there are those who go the extra mile and put on a big spectacle. But not every engagement is as joyous and celebratory. For various reasons, popping the big question and sharing news with loved ones can be a rather delicate situation, as Saira knows only too well.

As a Muslim woman, Saira grew up in a family that expected her to have an arranged marriage. 'I was brought up being told, "If you ever marry outside it's going to bring real problems; it'll bring shame on the family,"' she recalls. 'When I was at university, mum would call me back home from time to time and I'd be like, "Mum, what am I coming back for?", to which she'd say, "Oh, it's something really important." Then, when I was home, she'd say, "Can you go upstairs and bring this tray of food to these people in the room?" And then it clicked that she was trying to show me off.'

But as we all know, Saira is a modern and independent woman, and unbeknown to her family she had already met Steve, who was at the same university. Hitting it off straight away, they slowly got to know each other and even started living together without her mother's knowledge.

'I led this secret life because I was marrying outside my culture, outside my religion,' she says. 'I knew the only man I would bring home would be the man I was going to marry, so I had to be really sure this was going to last. So I led this secret life for three years and then finally I knew Steve was The One, and I had to take him home to meet my mum.'

As expected, Saira's mum didn't take the news all that well to start with, so when it came to Steve actually popping the question it wasn't quite as joyous as most brides-to-be would wish for.

'My mum went through a whole wailing process, "Oh, she's marrying a white man, oh my God!"' Saira remembers with a smile. 'The sad thing for me was when Steve did propose to me, I was so happy, but I had to say to him, "I've got to tell my mum first." But now he's the number-one son-in-law and can't do anything wrong.'

Although everything is hunky-dory now with Steve and her mum, Saira does say she regrets one thing about their very British wedding day. 'For my mum...obviously she had visualised the kind of wedding she wanted for me – you know, the sari, the gold, the henna – but I didn't have any of that. I had the big meringue wedding.'

Though she says her mum has never expressed any unhappiness about Saira and Steve's wedding day, Saira is convinced that she is harbouring some disappointment and says she would one day like to make it up to her mum and organise another wedding ceremony.

'She can't relate to a strapless dress in white, this has nothing to do with her culture,' Saira explains. 'I did that for me. But now she's getting on, she's 78, and I think I would actually like to do that for her. I just have this vision of me coming down the main road in Oxford on an elephant, Steve on a horse, the bhangra, all my girls in a sari doing their best light-bulbs dance! I'd love to do that.'

Saira adds, 'I'd like my kids to see mum does have a different culture, that she had a different part of her life. They don't really see that very often, because we don't live within that community,' she explains. 'Saira's Bollywood bhangra wedding here we come!'

Nadia admits that while she can remember proudly walking pregnant up the aisle six months after meeting Mark, she can't for the life of her recall deciding to get married in the first place. 'We were mad for each other at the start, but we just don't remember how we decided to get married,' she says. 'Once we did an article for this magazine and they said, "How was the engagement?" so we made it up as we went along! And sometimes now when we're at dinner parties Mark will say how we got engaged, and we'll get home and I'll say, "You do know that's a lie now that you believe." It's become our truth!'

While marriage is the goal in life for many women, Kaye says that the big day and all that goes with it has never really been her thing, even when she was a little girl. 'I can honestly say, hand on heart, I never did dream about a big white wedding,' she says. 'And because Ian is to a certain extent a bit beatniky and thought of himself as being unconventional we just didn't. And then by the time you have kids, it's just not as important.'

She says that she doesn't think either of her daughters are that fussed that their parents are not wed. 'I don't think either is bothered,' she says. 'Though my younger one would probably really enjoy the big day, but only because she would want to be the star of the show and elbow me on the way down the aisle, and I would end up in the bloody back of the pews and she would be in front of me!'

HOW TO HAVE A
STRESS-FREE WEDDING

Many of us spend years planning our big day. Some of us even start working out the details when we're kids, dreaming of that fairy-tale ceremony and slipping into that princess dress. But no matter how hard you plan your big day, nothing will stop some of us from working ourselves up into a ball of stress in the lead-up to the day. You've spent years dreaming about this amazing day and you want it to go off without a hitch. Many of our Loose Women, however, found ways to get through the day stress free, even if there was a little drama.

When Coleen got hitched to her now ex-husband Ray she says she was pretty relaxed. 'I didn't get stressed at all actually, because someone else organised mine,' she says. 'People were going, "Oh, what are your flowers like?", and I said, "I don't know, someone chose them." The only thing I wanted to choose myself was the dress, but for everything else I just trusted my friends who were doing it.'

While most brides would be keeping an anxious eye on what was going on around her, Coleen says she didn't worry about a single thing. 'I enjoyed every minute of it,' she exclaims. 'There was nothing I would have changed.' However, by the evening, some of the guests who'd particularly enjoyed themselves were getting a little rowdy. 'There was one guest in particular who was absolutely blotto,' Coleen recalls, 'and I remember my mother-in-law, who was 87 or something at the time, was sitting in a chair enjoying herself when this woman decided she was going to jive with her! She grabbed her by the walking stick and dragged her onto the dance floor. We jumped to the rescue and had to graciously put this woman in a taxi home as she was so drunk she couldn't see.'

Jane also took a back seat on her wedding day so that her hubby-to-be Gary could take control. And take control the senior music man did. 'I married someone who strives for perfection,' Jane laughs. 'He organised the whole thing. I just had to buy a dress. But on the night before the wedding, he gave me one job. He said that he had compiled a special tape for the day, with stuff like Ennio Morricone on it, and he put it in my handbag and told me to bring it along.

'As we know, all women change their handbag, so I got to the register office and realised I'd left the tape at home. Gary wasn't happy but knew we couldn't do anything about it, so when the registrar piped up and said he had music he reluctantly agreed. So in the end I walked down the aisle to "Love Changes Everything" by Michael Ball. When I joined Gary at the front of the room, he whispered to me, "I am going to kill you." He still goes on about it to this day.'

Like Jane and Coleen, Nadia was barely involved in the planning of her special day. In fact, she happily admits she was totally clueless.

'I didn't know a single thing happening at my wedding,' she laughs. 'The only thing I was in charge of was the dress. I had one specially designed as I was pregnant. I left the wedding, the marquee, the food, the flowers, *everything*, to my mum and my sister... The only thing I said – because we met on a show – was I'd like one of those little director chairs and a presenter chair, like you see on a movie set, to top the cake and I'd like it in fresh, bright colours. Everything else, I just left up to them. But when I walked into the marquee, the first thing I saw was yes, this little director chair and this tower of cakes, but they were in brown, beige and cream. Which aren't the colours of pretty flowers, are they? But that's how hands-off I was, I didn't know what I was having.'

However, before the ceremony, she had to deal with the added drama of a missing fiancé. 'Mark was a bit late and I was outside having a look to see where he was,' she remembers with a grin. 'Then his car pulled up and he fell out of the door looking dazed and confused. Out of the other door came his ex! Yes, she'd come in the car with him as we'd all been at the house first. It turns out that her car hadn't turned up – so she had jumped into the same one as Mark, the one that I had organised as a surprise for him.'

Thankfully, Nadia saw the funny side. 'The poor man was so beside himself that all I felt was sorry for him, because I knew that it hadn't been, "Oh, I want my ex in the car with me." I think she'd had a couple of drinks, and sort of got in the car by accident, and so he was like, "Nothing to do with me!"'

Once she got her hubby settled in the church, more drama followed, albeit joyous drama. 'When I got down to the end of the aisle, I turned round and announced to everyone that I was pregnant, which was a good moment. You could hear a pin drop and Mark was sweating, it was great.'

Nadia decided to play a little trick on her new husband to teach him who was in charge! 'On the way out, we walked back down the aisle with "Dancing Queen" blasting. You see, he hates ABBA. So as we were walking down the aisle, I said to him, "There you go,

I'm always going to be boss!"'

As you'd expect, Janet's wedding stories – and don't forget she's had her fair share of those – are irresistibly compelling. While there was no stress on the big day itself, the morning after one of them was another story.

'I'd been living with this guy for two years and I really, really adored him,' she recalls. 'Then we decided to get married and had a big wedding bash. It was an excellent party, loads of friends came and we all had fantastic time. The next morning, I got up and started to wash the kitchen floor. I turned to him and said, "Well, that was a mistake!" And he replied: "Yes, I agree!" Looking back, I think the wedding was just an excuse for a big party.'

Janet also provided her sister with a whole heap of wedding stress. 'My own sister didn't want me to be bridesmaid at her wedding! The thing is, she wanted a wedding in a church with the veil, the dress and everything else. What she didn't want was Janet walking up the aisle behind her in a kind of bridesmaid's dress... My mother said, "She doesn't want you to be a bridesmaid," so I said, "Fair enough." So when it came to the day, I wore a Zandra Rhodes couture outfit with a long coat. In the wedding photos my sister is looking really nice in the frock and her husband's got a nice suit on, mum, dad, the in-laws, and then there's me – "Oh my God, who's this Martian?"'

So when it comes to wedding stress, most of us are tough enough to deal with it, but what happens when something terrible goes wrong? Sometimes it can be as simple as a bad 'hair don't' or when the bride is forced to walk down the aisle with a bouquet that looks like a bunch of vegetables. Or, sometimes, it can involve a night in the cells. Eek!

'I think all of us have had the bad wedding hairdo!' Janet says. 'For some reason, on our wedding day, really strong-willed women like us allow a hairdresser to put something on our heads that we will never wear again! And you're walking down the aisle and the bloke's at the other end and he looks at you and says, "Who are you?" Then you look back at the photos and all you can say is,

"What the hell happened?'"

Jane's wedding was a jamboree of mini-dramas. Not only had she forgotten to bring Gary's ceremony-music mixtape along to the bash, she was also horrified to discover that her precious bouquet of lilies that she'd spent time preselecting were not quite as chic and as stylish as she had hoped.

'In my head,' she recalls, 'my bouquet was going to be a bohemian, slightly wild, unconstructed affair. But when I opened the box my heart sunk... Before I could say anything, Gary saw them and piped up, "Have you been to the allotment? They look like leeks." And they did. They looked terrible.'

But a dodgy-looking bouquet was the least of her worries. As unbeknown to her, her big day had been in danger of not taking place at all after her husband-to-be had been thrown into a cell.

'We decided to be a bit traditional by staying in different places the night before,' Jane explains. 'I'd stayed at home while Gary was in a hotel down the road with my mum and the kids. But when Gary turned up to the register office, the first thing I said to him was, "God, you look a bit rough!" I thought he'd been on a bender the night before, but when after the ceremony he explained what had happened, I nearly died!'

It turns out that in the early hours of the morning, the fire alarms at the hotel had gone off. In his haste to get out of the room, Gary – unable to find a dressing gown – had rushed to the foyer covering himself in just a flannel. Noticing that his kids and mother-in-law were nowhere to be seen, he demanded the receptionist call their room, the number of which he couldn't remember. The receptionist insisted that Gary head outside to the car park as per the fire drill but Gary, worried that his family could be caught up in a potential inferno, refused to budge and demanded angrily that the receptionist find his family pronto.

'Gary was in a right state,' Jane continues, 'and let rip at the man. "Is it a fire? I need to know where my kids are!" But the receptionist kept urging him to go to the car park with the other guests. But Gary wasn't having any of it and kicked off, throwing a rack of leaflets to the floor in a fit of temper. It then emerged that it had been a false alarm and everyone was allowed back to their rooms. But an hour after getting back into bed there was a knock on his door and four policemen walked in, arrested him and threw him in a cell. He tried to explain that he was getting married in the morning, but the police just laughed and said, "That's what they all say."

'Luckily, he was released half an hour before the ceremony, which is why he looked terrible. As he told me on the way to the reception he begged, "But don't tell my mother!"'

But of course, no matter how stressful a wedding can get, there's always one way of easing the tension. Or at least, there used to be...

Once upon a time, the wedding night would be the first time a devoted, loving and oh-so-pure couple would finally get to, er, *really* know each other! Of course, for most of us, that's not the way it works any more. So do couples, exhausted and tiddly after their big day, still factor in a bit of rumpy-pumpy on the night to officially consummate their marriage?

'I had sex three times on my wedding night!' a beaming Coleen laughs, confirming that some brides do indeed want the icing on the cake with a cherry on top. 'I remember it well because that's the last time we did it! But yes, we did it twice that night and then once in the morning.'

Jane, on the other hand, says memories of the latter part of her wedding day are vague. 'I *genuinely* can't remember, because quite a lot of alcohol was consumed that day!' she blushes. 'I don't think it really matters though; we aren't living in *Pride and Prejudice* days any more, where it's your first experience. Most of the time, you're already living with somebody, so I don't really understand the significance of it.'

IS IT EVER OK TO TAKE OFF YOUR WEDDING RING?

Saving yourself until your wedding night might not be seen as de rigueur these days, but are other marriage traditions still being upheld? For example, is it still important for a couple to wear their wedding rings at all times? Or does it matter if we slip them off every so often? Do we still believe that a diamond sparkler or solid gold band wrapped around our fingers represents the sanctity of marriage? Does it offer us a sense of belonging and a stronger bond with our loved ones? Or does it make it feel like we are owned by our hubby?

'I cannot bear to be without it,' Gloria says. 'I find it a great symbol. It's not that I was desperate to get married or anything like that. I didn't have to get married, but I think it's important. My husband Stephen lost his wedding ring once in the shower after losing a bit of weight, and I was so upset because he wasn't wearing his ring that I went out and bought him another one!'

'For me, it's important to keep your wedding ring on,' Coleen agrees. 'However, when my sister Bernie died, one of the side effects I got through having stress was eczema on my hands. I had never had it before; it was awful. As I result, I was forced to take it off. What amazed me was, at the time, I was working on *This Morning* and the first day I was on without the wedding ring, the emails that came through: "Why isn't the wedding ring on?" I thought, "How boring am I that they're just looking at my wedding finger?!" It is really important to me and I hate not having a wedding ring on.'

Nadia says, matter-of-factly, 'It doesn't symbolise anything for me, my ring or Mark's ring. I love being married, I love him and I know he loves me: "Never force them into the labour room and never force them to wear a ring."'

Nadia adds that the idea of wearing a ring can give people the outdated impression that a woman is seen as the 'property' of a man.

'I think if you *want* to, then that's fine,' she says. 'I think if it becomes a "thing", then it feels like it's "stamped" and it's like ownership. I don't want to be owned. I want to love and be loved. I didn't get married for the ring. I got married because I love him and because he loves me – I don't see my ring being part of that love.'

While Gloria says she likes 'the sense of belonging', Nadia says that even if Mark were to lose his ring, it wouldn't devastate her. 'If he took his ring off tomorrow I wouldn't think, "Oh my God, there's something wrong with our marriage." I'm just not superstitious about it,' she says. 'I trust him, I don't think he needs to go out with a ring on that says, "Keep your hands off!" It's up to him to live and behave like a married man.'

CAN WHIRLWIND MARRIAGES WORK?

Over the years we have seen many celebrities get swept up into a whirlwind romance and rarely did any of these shotgun relationships last, suggesting perhaps that couples should really put the work into their relationship before they decide to make a very serious commitment. But then, on the other hand, we have our very own Nadia and Mark, who married each other within six months of meeting and are still as happy today as they were back then, in spite of various bumps in the road.

'I think now we're stronger than we ever were but it does take a lot of work,' Nadia reflects. 'There's no way I knew him before I got married so I'm going to say something controversial now... I think if you did actually get to know somebody, you probably wouldn't marry them!'

What? Surely our Nadia isn't saying she regrets getting hitched? No, of course she's not, but she explains that the early stages of their relationship were deceptive because she and Mark were swept up in the first throes of mad young love.

'When Mark and I got married we were still in that phase where we were getting drunk and having fun. We were still in the romantic world,' she laughs. 'When we decided to get married it was a real leap of faith – we really didn't know each other.'

It wasn't long after the marriage that Nadia discovered that there were aspects of Mark that she hadn't been aware of from the start.

'I joke now about us being drunk a lot at the beginning but it became clear to me after about a year and a half that Mark had a drinking problem,' she reflects. 'In fact, he had a massive drinking problem and eventually he went into rehab. He walked in himself, he asked for help and he got sober. That was 2002 and he's never touched another drink. Words cannot describe how proud I am of him. It is a gargantuan task to get, and to stay, sober.'

Nadia reflects on that difficult period and how it brought them closer together. 'He was in rehab for a month and I had to go in with him once a week. I had to sit in these sessions, and talk so openly,' she remembers. 'People knew me off the telly and would be sitting there watching me, and I'd be having to say everything to him and he'd be having to say everything to me. But with that month of him doing that, it felt like we were in a ten-year relationship because he'd had to be so honest with me and I had to be so honest with him.'

Even though Mark left rehab sober, Nadia admits that marriage still wasn't a bed of roses. 'We had to work really hard at our relationship... We had Maddie soon into our relationship, so in the best possible way, we had a child, so we had to make it work,' she explains. 'We loved each other, that was for sure, but also for me there was no option but to make it work.'

Although Mark will recognise Nadia as his rock during this tough time, Nadia is the first to praise her family for believing in their relationship from the outset in spite of the hurdles.

'My parents were the most supportive because they loved him, like all my family did,' she says with a smile. 'But I could tell there were a lot of people out there who were convinced that this was never going to work. But then you tell me not to do something, and I'm going to do it! So if anyone thought it wasn't going to work – I was going to make sure it was going to work. And it helped that we really loved each other.'

But if we think whirlwind romances could be hard, what about long-distance romances... can they really work? On paper, having a break from a partner can be a total godsend. After all, absence makes the heart grow fonder, right? But there is also a danger that the longer you spend time apart the more distant you and your other half will become. And then, before you know it, one of you finds themselves tempted...

Sadly our girls understand this situation only too well. When Coleen was married to Shane Richie, he played away while working in Manchester. 'He was meant to be up there for three months but he ended up staying there for eighteen months,' Coleen remembers. However, work, it turned out, was the last thing on Shane's mind. While Coleen remained in London, Shane had hooked up with an actress, something Coleen only discovered when somebody sent her an anonymous letter revealing all about the affair.

Devastated at the time, she eventually split from Shane when he continued to cheat, in spite of promising to change his ways. 'You grow apart. I had my life in London. He had his life. Shane would come home on a Sunday, and we didn't have anything to talk about. He was tired and fell asleep. I would then be grumpy! So for me it absolutely didn't work.'

Now, years later, Coleen has learned a very important lesson about living apart from a partner. 'If a partner wanted to go away to Australia for three months we would have to seriously think about it because I've been burnt by that situation before,' she says. 'However, when Ray used to be away for a couple of weeks, I would get so excited about him coming back – it was like, "Oh great, we're going to see each other."'

Gloria also agrees that being apart from each other can be damaging for a relationship. 'I believe that relationships have to be fed and I do accept that many people make it work successfully. But it's hard. When I was with my first husband I unexpectedly came to work in London for Radio 2, and unexpectedly he went to work in South Africa for six months... By the time he came back from South Africa things were different. Don wanted to go back to Northern

Ireland and I didn't, and so things just slipped away. So for me, and particularly at my stage in life, I wouldn't want to be away from Stephen any longer than a week.'

While Jane acknowledges that long distances can indeed eat away at strong relationships, she thinks that if someone is aware from the outset that their other half has a career that will take them away from home, they might find it easier to deal with. 'It is all about context and what you're used to as well. If you marry someone who is in the Forces, for example, then you're used to that and that's what you expect,' she says.

However, she says that having a sudden change in living situations really does throw a spanner in the works. 'You know when you have friends of a certain age, and they have young children, and they say, "We're moving to the country – my husband is going to get a little flat and he is going to stay in the city during the week." And, sure enough, there's a massive strain on the relationship because they've developed a whole social life without you, and vice versa. The points of commonality disappear.'

Kaye agrees with Jane that living apart means a couple will begin to live different lives. However, she doesn't believe that temptation is necessarily always a worry.

'There's temptation everywhere. I mean, you know you could lead the most regular life and sit at a desk every single day next to somebody who you fancied and might find yourself in the stationery cupboard,' she laughs. 'However, if you spend too much time apart, then I think you can start to lose certain ties you have. People who work offshore, or people in the army must have to work really hard – I think that would be challenging for the relationship because you have separate friends, you start eating different kinds of food and watching different kinds of TV shows.

'No matter how we like to think that romances are all very glamorous, at the end of the day, you know when it progresses it tends to be "in from work, knackered, what's for dinner, watch the telly". If you're unable to develop any kind of joint interests, and you find you always want different things, then everything's going to be a fight.'

Looking back to her early days with Ian, Kaye says that their relationship remained strong when he was away working as a tennis coach. 'When I first met Ian he would be away for months at a time,' she recalls. 'All through our relationship he's been away for weeks at a time. I worked in London and Manchester and Norwich, so I would be away Monday to Friday, which was the norm for me, so I didn't feel that I was constantly worried about him. I think it's about where your relationship is. If you're always going to be slightly nervous that they're going to go off with somebody else then it means there's a real tension in that relationship.'

As much as she loves living with Ian and sharing their lives together, she says that she strongly believes in both halves of a couple having their own independence. 'I never wanted to be in a relationship where I'm living in somebody's pocket,' she declares. 'Because I also really enjoy the other friendships in my life. It's really, really important to me to have other relationships that are meaningful. I remember when I was growing up, Linda and Paul McCartney would say they had never spent a night apart and every time I heard that I thought, that doesn't sound right to me, because I think you should be able to be independent within a relationship. And so that's always the way it was for me.'

DOES GETTING MARRIED CHANGE YOU?

Getting married is a major deal, no two ways about it. Not just because it takes a lot of organising, but because it means that you and your other half are, in the eyes of the world and the law, officially united. But does it really change anything? Do you feel any different the morning after the long day before? If you've been living with your loved one for years, perhaps even had a couple of kids, is there any point in getting hitched at all? After all, will it make you feel like a different person? Well, to some, it does.

'It's a really difficult thing to explain to someone, but you really do feel very different after getting married,' Coleen says. 'One of my sisters was with her partner for 22 years. She had a grown-up son and two granddaughters. And she said to me one day, "I guess I better get married now I'm a grandmother. But as we've been together 22 years, what's the point?" And I said to her, "It will feel different, I swear to you it does." And on her wedding day, she came up to me and said, "Yes, it feels different, I can't tell you how, but it does." It's true. Everything feels like it just slots into place.'

Janet, with four weddings under her belt, is in total disagreement with Coleen and believes there is way too much importance placed on marriage these days. 'I got married four times but I didn't turn into another person,' she says. 'When you fall in love with someone, that's the most important thing, and that's got nothing to do with getting married. I think we build up marriage too much and think that it is the answer to everything. And then people get married and think their lives are going to have a rosy glow, but that is rarely the case, especially when you consider that one marriage in every three ends in divorce. People have unrealistic expectations of marriage and it's better to be with someone you feel comfortable with and who you can be committed to and who you utterly trust.'

LOOSE LESSONS

- If you haven't spent years dreaming about your big day with the blancmange white dress, like Kaye, that's fine. Forging a strong relationship is much more important.

- If you want a stress-free wedding, get someone else to organise the whole shebang for you!

- When it comes to your wedding be strong and make sure that you stick to what you want it to be. It is your big day after all.

LIVING TOGETHER

SHOULD YOU SAY YES TO KEEP MARRIED LIFE SWEET?

Marriage can sometimes feel like a series of carefully negotiated compromises. And this means that to avoid an argument, we may find ourselves biting our lip and agreeing with our fella just for a bit of peace. Do you sometimes find yourself saying 'yes' in order to keep things calm? Or do you stand your ground like Jane?

Jane says she never gives in if she thinks she's got a point. 'Like most couples we argue about silly things,' she says, 'but it could be something tangible. Like I'd tell Gary a film wasn't on in the cinema a certain week and he would say, "Yes it is." And then when I'd prove him wrong, he'd say, "Why do you always have to be right?" But why should I say yes and agree when the evidence is there? When it comes to having an opinion on something, I say "we have to agree to disagree" and move on. I mean, if you have an opinion, why should you change that? It's something long held and part of your make up.'

Kaye, meanwhile, says that she and her partner Ian rarely row, which surprises many of her mates. 'There are times that I will be pretty strong, but Ian and I really don't argue much at all,' she explains. 'It's not always healthy as I think sometimes there are things that we probably should be discussing. But neither of us enjoys confrontation at all. We're both really uncomfortable with it and we would rather avoid it.'

Kaye admits that she knows that the way she and Ian deal with problems is different from the way her friend Nadia does, which normally involves 'a good old flare-up, where she is screaming and shouting and all the rest of it'. 'She'll tell you she finds that quite a healthy thing in a relationship,' Kaye says. 'It blows away the cobwebs.

But for me, I don't think it works because I think things can be said in anger that are very difficult to get back. But I think I'd be the one to say, "Right come on, I really was unhappy with that – that really did make me feel rubbish." I would be the one to do that, but Ian is much better at saying sorry and trying to move on. I find that more difficult.'

Nadia says that she does say 'yes' occasionally to keep the peace, but is actually rather devious in the way she does it. 'In Mark's room, he has a cushion on his chair that says "Mrs Always Right",' she laughs. 'It was given to him to remind him – not by me – that I am always right. He says he's so glad to have it because he knows I am right most of the time. So he's very clever.'

'Anyway, sometimes, he acquiesces when we argue because fundamentally he knows I am right. But sometimes I will think, "Bless him, it's been so long since he's been right," and so I will say to him, "You're right," and then I will log it and store it in my head. Then I will somehow recreate the discussion or the argument a few weeks later and show myself as right. He has no clue about this. But he's happy!'

However, Saira says that as she has got older she no longer feels the need to appease her hubby to keep the peace. 'I have built myself to be a financially and emotional independent woman,' she says. 'I am the product of my upbringing, where I was controlled for a lot of my life. I had to say yes to things I didn't want to, culturally. But then I realised I didn't want to be like that for the rest of my life and when I lost my dad at 28 years old I thought to myself, life is too short to be doing things that you don't want to do.'

However, in spite of this, she is aware that she needs to show Steve that she is willing to work with him. 'You have to compromise, otherwise it's not a marriage,' she muses. 'Otherwise you're just two people who live separate lives and are sharing a mortgage. But there are women out there who try to please their man because they don't have the financial independence to go it alone. And that's sad. But Steve likes me the way I am. People say "poor Steve" because I am so vocal and because I don't take any rubbish. But Steve wouldn't have it any other way. The reason he likes me is because I challenge him intellectually and that I am not a walkover.'

ROWING IN PUBLIC

As we all know, our Loose Women love to voice their opinions, but Nadia admits that when she has something to say to hubby Mark, she's probably much more vocal than she should be and she doesn't mind where she does it.

'If I'm hormonal, whether premenstrual or perimenopausal, I find it really hard to control myself,' she says of her temper. 'Mark and I are both Scorpios; we are very passionate, very fiery, very happy still, after 15 years. But my God, when we row! I really row! He'll be going, "Not now! Don't say that here. People are looking!" And he'll remind me, "You're off the telly you can't do this!"'

But Nadia confesses that when she's on one there is no off switch, which can lead to some outrageous displays of behaviour. 'When I go, I just flip!' she explains. 'I'm very fiery – I'll jump out of the car and he's going, "Please, please, let me pull in!" and I'm saying, "Noooo, stop now!" If I get too crazy I have to jump out, I have to get away, and then I try and run down side streets, but he follows me and he'll slow up and says, "People are going to think I'm a weirdo," and I'll shout back, "That's because you are a weirdo! Leave me alone."'

Although Nadia assures us that after their many spats, she and Mark have a good laugh about all the wicked things they say to each other, she does admit that sometimes their behaviour means they can't return to the scene of the crime.

'There was this one time we were in a really fancy Heston Blumenthal restaurant in a hotel and having a row,' she recalls. 'Mark was facing out to the rest of the restaurant while I had my back to the swing doors to the kitchen and so I felt quite safe in my rage. I was perimenopausal and I'd had three glasses of rosé, by accident. Mark said something that didn't sit well with my hormonal state, and I went off on one and just didn't stop. The whole time he was ashen, and his eyes were popping and begging for me to stop! Now I can't go back to that restaurant from shame, and I love that restaurant.

What an idiot I am!'

Nadia is keen to assure us that she's definitely not always such a hot head! 'We're not like this all the time – the rest of the time I'm lovely!'

The idea of having a massive public barney puts the fear of God into Coleen. 'I love a good discussion. I'll talk about something if there's a problem, but I hate screaming and shouting,' she explains. 'As soon as somebody starts shouting at me, I'm not listening.'

During her marriage to Ray, her ex, she says that when they had an argument, she was very good at putting on a strong face while her husband made it quite clear that he was in a mood.

'I've always been good at hiding the fact we had a row if people came round,' she says. 'Whereas Ray, if he wasn't talking to me, then he was wasn't talking to anyone. It didn't matter if the Queen turned up. He would sit there blanking people. And then I'd be overcompensating. Meanwhile, our guests would leave the house thinking, "He's very close to a nervous breakdown!"'

Hard as it may be to believe, even cool-as-a-cucumber Jane has endured the occasional domestic in front of a crowd of people. 'Gary and I don't actually argue that much in public, but one night we went to a restaurant and it was supposed to be a really nice night, but then suddenly this argument just came out of nowhere,' she recalls. 'It got quite noisy and I became very aware that everybody on all the other tables had suddenly stopped eating and were all pretending not to listen! It was so embarrassing. Every time we drive past the restaurant now, Gary goes, "That's the place where we had that really big argument." "Yes, I know!" I'll say.'

Although Jane says she wouldn't want generally to bicker in front of her daughters, she thinks it can be beneficial for them to see their parents squabble. 'I wouldn't have a big, full-on row in front of them, it's very stressful. So I try to avoid that, but I think it's quite important for them to see parents falling out, having a resolution and talking again,' she says. 'I think it's important for my daughters to see me standing up for myself. So, if I feel that he's said something that

I don't like, I'll have a little snipe and then he'll have a little snipe back. They're not sitting there thinking, "Oh my God, they're going to get divorced!" They just kind of go, "They're arguing again!"'

SHOULD YOU KEEP ROMANTIC MEMENTOES FROM PAST RELATIONSHIPS?

Once we've mourned a relationship and finally moved on from it, should we cut ourselves off from the past entirely and never look back? And when we embark on a fresh, new relationship, how might our new love feel if we held on to keepsakes that reminded us of those times gone past?

Kaye admits that even though she's been with her partner Ian for years, she has still held on to certain memories from previous relationships. 'I've got love letters from my first boyfriend. Cards and little things,' she says. 'The ring that I wear on my wedding finger was from I guess what you would call my first love. I told Ian but he's not that interested.

'We've all had happy times in our lives, and life goes on, and you go through different stages,' she reflects. 'That was a wonderful first relationship that I had, although it didn't end so well! But I have lovely memories of that time so why not have the ring?'

Nadia says she is impressed that Ian has been so cool about Kaye's past, because she remembers having a former boyfriend who found it very hard to deal with the fact she had had a past. 'This one boyfriend I had years ago was a really lovely guy, but he was very jealous,' she recalls. 'One day I discovered that he'd gone through the house and had thrown away all my photos from my past.

'I remember being so upset because I used to do these Italian exchanges when I was a kid, I used to go over to Italy and they would swap over. Amazing life-forming parts of my life, you know. I had little flirtations and little holiday romances. And he had thrown them all away. ALL GONE! Just because he couldn't bear the thought of me ever having a past.'

When Gloria got divorced from her husband, her lawyer gave her some sage advice: 'He said to me, "Always keep the communication lines open, because there will always be births, deaths and marriages." How right he was.'

CAN THE WOMAN BEING THE MAIN BREADWINNER DAMAGE A MARRIAGE?

In the last few decades, there has been a significant shift away from the traditional family set-up, where women stayed at home looking after the kids while men went out to work as the main breadwinner. Nowadays the balance has shifted and not only are women returning to the workplace and often putting more emphasis on their careers, but more and more men are taking time out of work to be the main carer in the family, too. But can this reversal of the old ways cause problems within a happy marriage?

Janet says she thinks women becoming the main income provider could potentially spell trouble for a happy marriage. 'What's really interesting is that more women than ever are now the breadwinners and that will place an incredible strain on relationships, whether the woman wants it or not,' she says. 'You'll be the one who's earning more money than your husband or your partner – and when you go home and your partner's been at home all day, you've got to be pretend that you're interested in what they've done and you've got to downplay what you've done. I think it's very, very difficult.'

She adds that she thinks money tends to be the problem that can cause cracks in a relationship. 'I think money can cause a tremendous amount of problems – it's like the elephant in the room. It's a subject you never talk about and I think for men it is worse to deal with if their wives or girlfriends are earning more than them. It can emasculate them.'

Coleen agrees that even in these more progressive times some men can feel a little inferior if their women are in financial control. 'No matter how much you think we have moved forward with equality, the natural instinct of men is that "men are hunters",' she comments. 'And I think that most men find it emasculating when the wife is earning the money.'

In the early days of her relationship with ex-husband Ray, Coleen says he had trouble dealing with the fact that she was the one bringing in the most dosh. 'When we first met, he had a terrible problem with that. He hated it, not in a way in which he would take it out on me or we'd have terrible rows, but he understood the situation and didn't like it.'

She says she would feel sorry for Ray because sometimes he felt a little helpless. 'I would come home tired from work and say, "I wish I could win the lottery so I could stay at home and just do the kids and do this and that," but that would totally frustrate him because he would say, "You're doing everything; I want to go out and earn the money."'

Coleen says she thinks men have a much harder time dealing with this kind of situation and have difficulty expressing themselves about it, because they feel they might sound like they're telling women that we 'should be at home with the kids'.

Similarly, Jane thinks some women have to put on a show when they get home from a long day's work in order to keep their other half chipper. 'You don't pretend it's not going well,' she says, 'but you downplay what you've done. And the fact is you work really hard and you come home and you feel like you can't say, "I've worked hard!" There will be a lot of women watching the show who are working really hard. They might be on shift work, they might work in hospitals or in shops, and then they go home and have got to pretend it wasn't hard work and be interested in the other half.'

HOW OFTEN DO YOU FEEL LOVE FOR YOUR PARTNER?

While there are times when we feel blissfully happy with our partner, there are other moments when we absolutely don't. But does that mean we love them any less than we did before? Or do we sometimes feel like our other halves don't love us as much as we love them? And is it actually natural not to love your partner sometimes?

Coleen says she doesn't think it's realistic to love your man all the time. 'If you were to ask me, do you love your partner 100 per cent of the time – then the answer would be NO. I think we feel love in different forms all the time. Sometimes I would say to Ray, "Love you? I don't even like you!" But that doesn't mean I didn't still love him and I would have been there if anything happened.'

Jane agrees and says she believes that while – deep down – love is constant within a relationship, sometimes circumstance can affect the way we feel about our partners at a given moment. 'I think love is always there as the underlying emotion, but there are days when I just think to myself, "Grrr, you're literally driving me to insanity!"' she muses. 'But then, if, God forbid, something happened to him or somebody was attacking him, I would be there for him in a flash. It's there underneath the whole time.'

When it comes to how much our other halves are loving us back, our ladies aren't quite so sure what to think.

'When I was with Ray, I didn't always know that he was as in love with me as much as I was with him,' Coleen says. 'Ray was really shy and felt self-conscious about emotionally opening up. The only time I knew he loved me was when someone had hurt me or upset me and he said he wanted to "kill" people and then I'd think, "Oh, he really does love me." But did he say "I love you" every day, or "You look amazing" or leave me a little note? The answer is no. If he had left me a note, I'd have thought he was up to something! He just wasn't that type of person.'

LOOSE LESSONS

- Want to keep the peace with your fella and be supportive? Let him (sometimes) think he's in the right – even when he might not be!

- It is OK if sometimes you are irritated by your man. It doesn't mean you love them any less.

- Your family structure should follow whatever makes you both happy. Don't feel you have to stick to traditional roles. However, you know a happy wife equals a happy life.

AFFAIRS

IS MONOGAMY UNREALISTIC?

 As gorgeous and wonderful as your other half is, are you truly content to have sex with him and only him for the rest of your long life?

It will come as no surprise whatsoever that Janet is not exactly a big believer in monogamy and has enjoyed the company of a number of men over the years. 'I've never placed any great store by fidelity, because I think the main thing is to have a soulmate, an intellectual partner, someone who you feel comfortable with as a person in their brain and physically...I think it's overrated,' she asserts. 'And certainly during marriages, I found it quite hard to be faithful, and there was a period in my life where I had "back-burner men", "front-burner men", whatever.'

Janet adds that those who think people have affairs because they're insecure or need some kind of validation is 'rubbish'. 'I had affairs,' she announces unashamedly. 'I just fancied them.'

Kaye is flummoxed by Janet's view of fidelity, admitting: 'Janet is a very unique individual. I feel a bit sorry for people who can never get past the first stage and carry on into a long-haul relationship, because that's where I think the real goodies are. Having said that, if you don't want that and you want to sort of keep your own space; you want the frisson and you just want that initial bit, then that's your choice. It wouldn't be my choice.'

Coleen, meanwhile, thinks that men tend to enter into an affair far more easily because looks play a large part in who they're sexually attracted to. 'It's harder for men to stay monogamous. Men are much more visual,' she says. 'If I were to have an affair it would be because I really fancied the guy or there were things really bad in my marriage and I was looking for that emotional connection... But for men, its visual. It's more about sex.'

However, Janet disagrees with her panel-mate. 'So, Coleen, you're saying women and men judge each other, select each other, based on women seeking a sense of humour and all different things, whereas men are going on looks. Speaking as someone who has not been terribly faithful in their life, I just think people are different.'

But Saira is at odds with Janet and admits she finds it hard to understand her thought process.

'I am shocked that Janet is so confident about saying, "I was married to so-and-so and I had an affair with him." I think she is brave to be so open and honest, but my take is that if you are in a relationship then you are in a relationship. If you want to be with somebody else then talk about it and move on. And if you want to be with millions of people, then just be single and sleep around.'

Saira says the very idea of cheating on someone simply doesn't sit well with her. 'I would feel guilt and betrayal,' she says. 'I wouldn't feel like a good person. As humans we know our own laws, we understand that there are limits we tend to abide by. We think and choose. So why do you choose that behaviour? If we were all cheating there'd be a lot of unhappy people and I think we'd all lose faith in human nature. If you are with someone you should show trust and respect. I have no problems with people having more than one partner, but people need to know where they stand. I am up for open relationships. But when people are playing away without their partner's knowledge, I find that harder to deal with.'

ARE ONE-NIGHT STANDS FORGIVABLE?

If your other half confessed that he had had a drunken one-night stand, how would you react? Would you explode and kick him out, or would you stay calm, admire his honesty and be thankful that it was a one-off? Is a one-night stand as damaging to a relationship as a fully fledged affair? Or is it just a slip-up that can be forgiven if the guilty party is truly sorry?

On the other hand, are you the one who has got so tiddly on a night out that you have let yourself get into a situation you wish you hadn't? Would you tell your partner what had happened or, as it was a drunken one-off, never to be repeated, would you keep your secret to yourself?

Coleen says she can feel for those individuals who might have drunkenly made a silly decision in their time. 'An affair is when someone, time and time again, is seeing someone else, usually for sex, almost as if they are living a double life,' she says. 'But then there are those guys and girls who get horribly drunk and do something they really regretted and keep it to themselves so as not to destroy their relationship, and then have to live with the secret, which must be hard. I still don't necessarily condone that, but sometimes people can get carried away and things happen.'

Janet thinks it's perfectly acceptable for a man or a woman to have one-night stands as much as they want and should be allowed to carry on doing so in secret, suggesting it is 'great for all concerned'.

Coleen vehemently disagrees and reminds Janet that while one half of a couple might be happily having it away with a hook-up, the other half is home alone and obviously oblivious to what is going on elsewhere.

In response, Janet says she believes that what someone doesn't know doesn't hurt them. 'I don't think a one-night stand is something that people regret!' Janet reasons.

Jane says she is unsure about how she would deal with Gary having a one-night stand. 'In theory, in my head, if it was a one-night-stand scenario on a business trip overseas, I would ask myself is that enough for me to pull the rug from under my kids' lives?' she muses. 'If it was an affair, then no. For me an affair – texting each other, the deceit – would just eat me up.'

Nadia says she thinks she could forgive Mark if he got carried away on a night out and made a meaningless, of-the-moment error of judgement. 'Everyone can make a mistake with a one-night stand,' she reasons. 'If you haven't planned to go out and be unfaithful and everyone's giddy or had too much to drink. That kind of scenario is not the same as someone who works with someone, and has been thinking about them, planning a liaison, taken them out for dinner. That's totally different. I think I'd work through it if Mark had a one-night stand. I know him so well, and have been through so much, just to throw it away on an accidental night. I could forgive him.'

In fact, Nadia goes as far as to say that she would actually feel more hurt if Mark, who has been sober for 17 years, fell off the wagon. 'I think it would be worse for me if he drank again than if he had an affair,' she explains.

Nadia says she can sympathise with those bewildered people who feel lost and isolated and who sometimes stupidly fall into the arms of another. 'I read a stat a while back that 10 per cent of expectant fathers cheat on their pregnant partners sometime during pregnancy,' she reveals. 'But if you think about it – or if I think about me, when I had my baby – I was deranged, I was deluded. I had my boob hanging out with something hanging off it that wasn't Mark; he was never going to see them again. The poor guy was on the back burner. But he was a good, solid man who stayed. But no one's perfect. Having a baby is the biggest shock of your life. It was nothing like I expected. Men are on the edge.'

Jane is fast to point out that a man's actions totally depend on the individual himself. 'It all depends on the man. When I had Grace, Gary was so in love with her... he almost looked at me like I was this amazing person who was looking after this baby.'

But like Nadia, Saira says that because of the length of their relationship, she would definitely try to work things out if Steve admitted to a one-night stand. 'As I am so confident about who I am, my relationship and my husband, I don't think that a one-night stand would put my marriage in jeopardy. I think we'd talk about it and I would ask why it happened. But I don't think it would be the end of the world. We are all human, we all make mistakes. Besides, I think a drunken one-night stand is different to being calculating and having an affair behind someone's back. But it has to be a one-off and not a regular thing – your guy shouldn't be saying, "Oops I did it again!"'

CAN A MARRIAGE SURVIVE AN ADDICTION?

Long-term relationships are never easy. While for the most part we will be deeply devoted to our other half, we can also expect all those lovey-dovey moments to be punctuated by disagreements. And that's only to be expected. But during your union, there will be many tough times that will pop up when you least expect them. If a relationship is strong, then there's a good possibility that you make it through. Sadly, sometimes something happens that will test a couple to breaking point, and will ultimately mean they decide to go their separate ways.

Not long after she and her husband got married, Nadia realised that Mark had a problem with alcohol and, with a baby on the way, she demanded he do something about it. 'I gave him an ultimatum,' she remembers. 'I said you will not spend another night in this house unless you get help for your alcoholism.

After completing a 28 day programme at the Priory and attending various meetings, Mark has now been sober for almost 20 years, but, as Nadia explains, it's not been an easy process. 'It's so hard, you do have to keep working at it all the time. Recently we were in the car, listening to a programme about alcoholism on the radio, and he just had to switch off and stop the car, and we both had a massive cry. And it just comes out of the blue, because you do have to work at it every single day to stay sober.'

Nadia says at the start of their relationship it took her a while to realise there was a problem. 'It was a couple of years before I realised that Mark wasn't just a party guy or a heavy drinker – he was an alcoholic,' she says. 'I was a party girl, so it was just like normal. I still drink, I love to drink, but there is a real difference between someone who drinks and someone who is an alcoholic.'

When it came to telling Mark he had to sort himself out, Nadia found herself struggling to cope. 'It's such a hard thing to be honest about, and to say that we've got a major problem here,' she recalls. 'It wasn't until Mark checked into the Priory that I had any awareness that I was enabling him. I'd never even heard the terminology before. It basically meant that I was supporting his alcoholism by covering for him. It was a huge shock to our friends and family when Mark went into rehab because nobody knew he was an alcoholic except for me. He was what is called a high-functioning alcoholic. He was still brilliant at his job and hugely entertaining in social situations.'

Although she knew she was being tough on her husband when she gave him the ultimatum to get help or get out, she admits that she never considered walking away from him. 'No matter what happened between us, I knew he had the most incredible heart of gold and the drinking was a symptom of other things, like depression. He was basically numbing himself with alcohol,' she says. 'But I also knew that I wasn't going to live with him if he carried on. He might not have survived.'

Once they started attending meetings, Nadia's involvement became so intense that she found herself distancing herself from her loved ones, including her best mate Kaye. 'We lost contact for three years,' she sighs, shaking her head. 'I feel really gutted about that, but if anybody's watching, man or woman, who's living with any kind of addict, they will know what I mean when I say it's so all-consuming. It's really exhausting. My heart goes out to everyone.'

Now Mark has been clean for almost 20 years and Nadia says their relationship is happier and more healthy than ever. 'We love each other dearly,' she reflects. 'We always will, till the day we die.'

Speaking about his recovery, Nadia's husband Mark says it has been a tough ride. 'Every day is a struggle. Every day is a huge effort,' he says. 'The whole day is to be attacked, to be grappled with, it's to be fought. It is exhausting. I always say to Nadia and the girls, "Look, you're all finding me irritating now; you can all walk through that door and leave me, I can't. I have to stay in the same room as me."'

Mark says that during his stint in rehab he was told by counsellors that you must push yourself for you, not for your family, but he's not sure he agrees. 'The most important thing they used to say in the Priory is you need to need to do it for yourself,' he shares. 'You're not getting sober for your wife, you're not getting sober for your children. But for me at least, it's bullshit. There's no better reason to get sober than for your wife and your children. I struggled to find a reason to do it for myself because I thought I could cope, I could carry on... The best reason is Nadia and the kids. That is what has worked for me.'

CAN A MARRIAGE SURVIVE AN AFFAIR?

So for our Loose Women, a one-night stand is potentially forgivable and – in theory at least – something that can be filed away as a regrettable mistake and eventually forgotten about. But what of a fully fledged affair? Could you forgive your other half if you found out he was having a long-term intimate relationship with another woman? Or could you ever imagine yourself embarking on an illicit fling with another man? Could your marriage survive the deception?

Coleen, who was cheated on by her first husband, Shane, is surprisingly open minded when considering what she would do if a partner were to do the dirty on her. In fact, she even thinks that sometimes a moment of madness could actually be beneficial for a relationship that's turned stale, as it would make you assess any underlying causes.

'I think it depends massively on the circumstances of the affair and what kind it is, as I do think there's a difference between a fully blown affair and a moment of madness,' she reasons.

Coleen knows of one couple where an affair has happened, and they went on to 'enjoy 30 more years of blissful marriage... They'd been childhood sweethearts and she found out her husband had had an affair. We were all so shocked at the time. And then we were even more shocked when we found out they had chosen to stay together and we were like, "How can she do that?"'

The couple went on to have marriage counselling, which helped them see where they had gone wrong. 'They worked out she'd become very wrapped up in the four kids,' Coleen explains. 'Her whole time was spent with the kids. He was always at work and they'd forgotten the reason why they were together. So they had loads of counselling, which brought them back. To this day they are so happily married... it worked for them. So I would say that some people can do that, and can become stronger.'

She adds that it also depends on who the person has had the affair with. 'There have been loads of instances where it comes out that it was the best friend or the brother or a sister-in-law! In that situation, it's tougher because that's two people who are close to you who have been deceiving you.'

Gloria says she would find it hard to forgive her husband if he strayed. 'For me, it has to be one on one,' she says. 'I could not live with somebody who said they wanted an open marriage or to have affairs. I cannot bear cheating on any level. And I can't bear people who tell lies, who don't keep their word.'

However, she can understand why some women will forgive their unfaithful partners. 'I guess it depends what the circumstances are, what age you're at, what stage you are in your life,' she muses. 'I think if I caught my husband cheating, I would just say OUT. That's it, over and done. You have to have trust, but trust can get broken. It's a terrible thing if you're still in love with somebody and they break that bond. But an affair is like a slight chip in a china cup. It's there, it's not a big thing at the beginning but then slowly but surely that little crack goes further and further and further down.'

She admits that if she were cheated on she would find it very hard to overcome. 'I don't think I could ever mend it sufficiently or get over it sufficiently to have a relaxed marriage,' she reflects.

Kaye agrees that letting go of a long relationship is not always easy and that if she were ever in that position a lot of thought would have to go into making the right decision for both parties.

'I think in a lengthy marriage or relationship there are credits and debits,' she explains. 'If I felt my partner had just completely lost it or was in a terrible place and I could rationalise why he had behaved the way he had, and if I felt there was enough good in our relationship to make it worth pursuing, possibly I could do it.'

Nadia says as she has become older and has formed a closer, richer bond with her husband Mark, her opinion on forgiving a cheating partner has changed.

'If you took me back a few years, I would have been mean and said to someone. "Right, get rid of him. Out the door. Lock the door." But you get older and these things change,' she says. 'When I look at my marriage, it's a hard graft, in lots of ways. Mark has often said to me, "How did you stay with me through those years when I was drinking?" And I told him, "Because I knew you were good, a deeply good, good person." And I still think that. And I think whatever he did I know that his soul is really good, and hope he feels the same way about me. We all make mistakes.'

But while the idea of discovering that your loved one has been sexually and emotionally intimate with another person is enough to bring your world crashing down around you, what is going through the mind of the person who is actively gallivanting around behind someone's back?

Janet explains, 'When I was married the first time, all those years ago, I was unfaithful. I was brilliant at lying, I could do an A level in lying. But my husband didn't find out until he followed us to our "love nest" in the New Forest and confronted me.'

She told him that she and her secret lover were merely conducting an interview, but her husband didn't buy it.

'He said I had two minutes to get in the car and if I did come back to London with him, our marriage would carry on and he'd forgive me,' Janet remembers. 'But I spent the first half of the two minutes arguing and then I went indoors to think about it and then he drove off.'

IS THERE EVER AN EXCUSE FOR HAVING AN AFFAIR?

Affairs can happen for many reasons. Sometimes, a man or a woman is highly sexed and, in order to feed their sexual appetite, they decide to look further afield. But sometimes an affair can be a cry for help from someone who is feeling neglected by their spouse, a feeling with which Coleen can certainly identify.

While she was married to Shane, the couple were living pretty much separate lives, a lonely period of time that led to Coleen making a very drastic and uncharacteristic life choice...

'I had an affair,' she confesses. 'I'm not proud of it and I don't condone it and to this day I'm still ashamed!'

However, Coleen says that having sex with another man helped raise her self-esteem. 'It was emotion based,' she reminisces. 'I had just had Jake and he was about eight months old. Shane was away working, doing really well. After a while, I just felt that he started to forget I was even there. I just felt so unattractive. Then I went away to work and some guy came along and made me feel like a million dollars. That's how it started.'

Even though she enjoyed her fling, and began to feel special again, she was filled with guilt. 'I'm not making excuses for it and I'm not recommending it because what I did ultimately just brings heartache,' she says. 'I always say now, if I ever feel the way did back then, before anything happened I would say, "This is how I am feeling and this is potentially what that could lead to."'

Jane says that she can see how dating apps could be tempting for folks who are dealing with a troubled relationship. 'I read about a woman who said that her marriage had been sexless for ten years. She said that she still loved her husband and that she used a certain site purely because she knows it will be no strings attached. I kind of sympathise with that.'

However, she also says she finds it hard to get her head around the fact some people will visit a site designed for 'cheating' that could ultimately wreck their relationships. 'I think that when you go on a website like this you are actively making a decision to put your marriage in jeopardy,' she sighs. 'I don't understand it, particularly for women, because I think when women have an affair it's because they're not getting any attention at home and somebody tells them they're attractive, and that raises their self-esteem. So I just don't understand women who just log on to a website and go, "Oh, I like the look of you, right let's meet in this hotel and have sex." Maybe I'm old fashioned!'

'I think these sites are a really cold way of having an affair,' Coleen comments. 'It's lazy. I mean, why can't they go out and meet someone and offer them a drink and then get together?! But instead, someone will just click a button and go, "Oh yeah, he or she'll have an affair with me." I think it's even more insulting if you were their other half and you found out about it.'

LOOSE LESSONS

- If you believe that monogamy is overrated feel free to have 'back-burner' or 'front-burner' men. Just be careful that it doesn't blow up in your face or that you hurt people with your actions.

- If you are worried that your man is dealing with an addiction, then you will need to confront him, help him and be there for him through thick and thin.

- Finding out that your partner is having an affair can be heartbreaking, but do look at the circumstances of it before you make your final decision on whether to leave them.

WHEN LOVE DIES

HOW DO YOU KNOW WHEN IT'S TIME TO GO YOUR SEPARATE WAYS?

Ending any relationship will be hard. There will be a significant moment in your life that leads you to finally come to terms with the fact that you have exhausted every possibility of saving what you think you have, and you decide enough is enough.

Coleen says that she remembers all too well the moment she knew the time was right to put an end to her marriage to Shane. Two years after she first discovered his infidelity, and had subsequently forgiven him and taken him back, she received a phone call out of the blue that helped her make one of the most important decisions in her life. 'The one thing that did it for me was when the mother of the girl he was cheating on me with phoned me up and said, "Do you know where Shane is?" I replied innocently, "He's away working," and she said, "No, he's on holiday with my daughter" – and all I could say in response was, "How lovely."'

Looking back, Coleen remembers she took the devastating news so calmly, soaked it in and made a decision that would change her life forever. 'It was that instant moment when I thought, "OK, that's it," and my heart shut down and I didn't feel pain or anything.'

Kaye agrees that there is always a 'moment of clarity' in a person's life that gives them the push they need to radically change their lives. And as one of the longest-serving Loose Women, Coleen has been through a lot over the years, losing her sister, tying the knot and opening up about a variety of personal issues that have affected her and her family. At the start of 2018, Coleen revealed on the show that she and, Ray, her husband of 11 years were calling time on their marriage. Although she has had a tough time dealing with the change in her life, she is aware that the decision had to be made for the happiness of both her and Ray, and of their daughter Ciara.

'We really, really did try to work things out,' Coleen says. 'We were never ones to just go, "Oh, we're having problems, let's call it a day." We've both tried but it just gets to a point where you think, "You know what? It's not working and we can't get it back together." It's not a failure to say we've tried – so we just decided to move on.'

Coleen says that being an agony aunt, offering readers advice on their own marriage woes, led her to realise that she ought to set about making her own life better. 'It is really sad, but break-ups happen, and instead of staying with someone because I was too scared of being on my own, I had to decide to make a drastic change,' she says. 'I'm nearly 53. I've kind of turned it round and thought to myself, it's just a new chapter and that's exciting in itself. I just couldn't sit here and lie.'

Coleen says that, looking back, she had a real sense that her relationship with Ray was in trouble over the festive period back in 2017. 'The New Year before I started divorce proceedings was a real light-bulb moment for me,' she recalls. 'We were having a New Year's Eve party and everyone was there. When the clock struck midnight, I looked at Ray and saw that he was going round the room hugging people and wishing them a happy new year. And, then, he came up to me and said, 'Have you got a fag?' Normally the first person you kiss or hug on New Year is your husband, your partner. It just wasn't there for us at that point. So I thought to myself, "Oh, we're just done."'

IS DIVORCE ALWAYS BAD FOR KIDS?

When you know the relationship is dead and there is no going back, it's time to start making plans to move on. But if there are children in the mix, then there comes that difficult moment when you have sit them down and talk to them about what is going to happen. While it is possibly one of the hardest moments in any parent's life, it is something that has to be done for the best interests of everyone.

Coleen says that when her marriage to Shane was swirling down the plughole, her boys Jake and Shane Jr – who were four and seven at the time – were blissfully unaware of all the dramas that were going on in the background. 'The good thing is we were still really friendly with each other,' she recalls, 'so the boys never saw us arguing or having a go at each other or anything like that.'

However, finding the words to explain to them what was happening didn't come easy, as she was worried about how the boys might react. 'I wasn't sure how they'd take it,' she explains. 'I guessed, because Shane Jr was quite reserved, he'd go off quietly for a couple of hours and sort it out in his head and then come back and might want to speak about it – or not – while Jake, I predicted, would go mental because he was a very emotional little boy.'

But deciding when it was best to tell the boys was taken out of Coleen's hands when a newspaper phoned her to inform her that they were running her marriage-split story on the front page the next day.

'I was being forced to tell them what was going on because Shane Jr was at school and I didn't want him to hear it from his friends,' she says. 'Because Shane senior couldn't face the boys, he told me I had to do the big chat. So I took both the boys upstairs and lay on the bed and told them that we were getting divorced. Jake took it remarkably well and it was Shane Jr, who I thought would be cool and quiet about it, who curled up into a foetal position and let out the most painful and heartbreaking noise that sounded like a wounded animal. It broke my heart in two.'

However, in her marriage with Ray, Coleen says it was when their daughter Ciara confided in her that she knew things weren't right between mum and dad that she finally felt ready to move on and start divorce proceedings, feeling assured that their daughter would be OK with the change in the family set-up.

'It was our daughter in the end who said, "Mum, it's not working. You need to make a decision, because it's not fair on any of us really, to live in that kind of atmosphere." So, in a way, it was Ciara herself who made me think, "Great, she's going to be all right if her mum and dad aren't together any more." She said to me, "Listen, mum, I love you and dad and I want you both to be happy. If you're going to be happier apart then that's OK. Please don't stay because of me.'"

However, Gloria says that when she divorced her first husband she wrote letters to her children Caron, Paul and Michael to try to explain why the marriage had gone wrong. 'I know for a fact that they have all kept their letters,' Gloria says. 'I would like to think that those letters were consoling for the kids at the time, but I can never be sure.'

IS A STRESS-FREE DIVORCE POSSIBLE?

So you know the marriage is over. You've tried your hardest to make a go of it, stuck a Band-Aid over the wounds, but have then come to terms with the fact there is nothing more that can be done. It's over. And so the next step is divorce. You might feel like you've let yourself down (and your kids, if you have any) – but if you think about it, in the long term, getting out of an unhappy marriage can sometimes be the best thing for everyone involved, as you can move on and find future happiness.

But getting divorced has not historically been an easy process as a couple had to wait two years before they were able to start proceedings, or one half had to point the finger at the other. However, in April 2019, the UK government announced plans to reform the divorce process to remove the concept of fault, which means unhappy couples can now finally have the opportunity for a stress-free divorce – which makes Janet very happy indeed.

'The old law encouraged a lying culture,' Janet explains. 'You have to admit fault if you want to get divorced in less than two years. So that meant that people all over the country were lying to get out of their marriages in less than two years. And if neither of you agreed to do it in two years you'd have had to stay together for five years, which is mad in the case of unhappy marriages. I have lied. I have been to court and made statements to get divorced that were lies because I wanted out of a marriage. I was never deterred because I wanted that person out of my life.'

So the passing of the new law, which will eradicate the need to blame a partner for the breakdown of the marriage, is music to Janet's ears.

'I really welcome these new laws,' she declares. 'Let's be honest, marriage for some people has run its course, and the old divorce law, which had been going for 50 years, is completely out of date. This idea that one person had to make up a load of allegations about the other, because the only way you'd get a divorce was to say there was a guilty party, and someone took the blame. Life's not like that, and it's so cruel if children are involved because children are going to hear all these things. The old laws invite people to tell lies, imply that their partner is violent or threatens violence. This is all absolutely disgusting and should have ended decades ago.'

Janet says she discovered for herself how difficult divorce actually could be after she wanted to end one of her marriages.

'When I got hitched in Las Vegas years ago, I mistakenly thought I could get divorced in Las Vegas just as quickly as I got married there,' she remembers. 'Then, to my horror, I discovered that under English divorce law, because my husband was English, we had to wait months and months, and there had to be a guilty party.'

Coleen agrees with Janet and says the awkward process of divorce has been hard for her and Ray. 'I think people who say divorce is easy have never been divorced,' she says. 'I don't think it's easy at all. And for them to say that you should really try and work at it, is just rubbish.

'In my case, I spent the last two-to-three years trying to work at our relationship. But there must come a time when you realise it is not working for either of you. I don't want to stay with somebody just because divorce is hard.'

Coleen adds that because she and Ray continue to be on really good terms, the idea of having to say negative things about each other for the divorce papers made the situation much harder.

'The marriage may have run its course, but we're still friends,' Coleen says. 'So we wanted to do it as nicely as possible. But then you have to go and give your reasons why you want a divorce. I was saying to my sister, "I haven't really got a reason, we're just not getting on and we've fallen out of love." But officially you have to give five reasons, so it wasn't just citing irreconcilable differences. So in the end I'm literally making them up. Then I had to phone Ray warning him about what he was going to receive through the post.'

HAPPILY DIVORCED

Not every divorce is bitter and nasty. Some marriages actually end on good terms, when those involved come to terms with the fact that the love they once shared is no longer there and just a platonic relationship remains. And that means, for the sake of your happiness, you have to make that break once and for all so that one day you and your partner can be happy all over again.

Janet is aware that there are many women who are living in unhappy marriages who feel like they would be failing if they were seen to be throwing in the towel. But she wants to encourage those insecure women to be brave and to be strong and take control of their destiny to ensure that their futures are bright.

'A lot of women, particularly of my generation, remain married to people because they're fearful,' Janet says. 'Fearful of living alone, fearful of how their old age will be. I always say to them, be brave, break out of it. Don't live with someone who you've lost all respect for, who you don't have sex with, who bores the backside off you. Please, please, please – have the guts. You can, you can.'

If anyone knows about how divorce can make you feel much happier then it's Coleen. Since she and Ray decided to end their 11-year marriage, Coleen admits the pair of them are now the best of friends.

'I think it is so easy to focus on everything that went wrong,' she says. 'I don't want to think about the moments there was sadness or we argued. I would rather focus on the great years because they were fantastic and we had Ciara. I have to focus on all the good because the bad has led us to splitting up. And, personally, it's the only way I can move forward and I think it's better.

'Since we said our relationship wasn't working and we need to split up, we've turned into the friends that I think we should have always been,' Coleen says with a smile. 'I mean, we're such good friends now. We're getting on great, we're making each other laugh again. This experience has made me realise that I always loved him as a friend, and over these last couple of years we forgot that. I think maybe we should have just stayed friends really.'

MOVING ON

So the marriage is over, and you have begun to pick up the pieces and think about what life is going to be like now. But what happens next? What can you expect from the future?

Life after a break-up or a divorce can be a pretty tough time for all parties. You feel vulnerable, alone, and the confidence you gained during the relationship seems to evaporate.

Coleen says that when she split from Shane she was left in a very insecure state. 'I was left thinking, "I don't know what to do now," as up until then we had had our future mapped out and kind of knew how it was going to be. But there I was, single, with kids, and I was left wondering if anyone would ever want to be with me and take on two kids,' Coleen recalls. 'But I think the real fear I felt was that I didn't want to go back out on the single scene and go to clubs or wine bars or shave my legs – actually I never went that far!"

Janet agrees and says that starting out again can be a pretty hard time for any woman. 'The idea of going on a date is frightening,' she says. 'When I got divorced the second time, which was my fault, I called up my ex who I was still on good terms with and told him that I felt like I couldn't go on a date because I had never really been on one properly, so I didn't know what to do. Previously, if I'd seen someone I liked and fancied them, then I'd have sex on the first date. If they were useless, then there wasn't a second date. So I said to my ex, "I need another partner," and he said, "Leave it with me." He called me back a couple of days later and told me he had a great bloke for me. He introduced me, we went for lunch and I eventually married him.'

But if you're worried about the prospect of love after love (thanks, Cher, for that catchy phrase), then take heed of Nadia's wise words. 'My experience has proved to me that we women can deal with break-ups a lot better than men can,' she says. 'I mean, we get right to the heart of our pain, and it's like cleaning out a wound, so you are not suppressing the pain any longer. So I think we women move on a lot better than men.'

LOOSE LESSONS

- If you're thinking about getting divorced, don't underestimate your kids' understanding of it. Talk to them honestly as you might actually find they already think it's a better idea for mum and dad to be apart.

- A divorce doesn't need to be a 'tit for tat' process. Try to keep your relationship as civil as possible as it will ensure the divorce moves quickly and smoothly.

- Moving on might not be as hard as you think. Don't focus on finding a new partner. The first step is to just get out there and start making new connections.

— ❤ —

PART 2
THE PARENT TRAP

The total and utter joy of finally bringing your little one into the world is indescribable. Not only are you relieved that the baby you are holding in your arms has safely arrived, but you also know that you've made it through that excruciatingly painful pushing and shoving stage. But in many ways that was a piece of cake compared to what lies ahead. Now you've got that babe in arms, the hard work really starts.

For the next 18 or so years, or at least until your little one has developed into a fully grown independent adult and moved out of home to embark on a life of their own, alongside all the joy that motherhood brings, there are the inescapable tough decisions and worry that go hand in hand with being a parent.

But like most things in life, being a mum takes practice, and we can put a lot of pressure on ourselves to get everything right immediately. Don't forget, you are of course dealing with a little person you've never met before, who has certain needs but who can't tell you what they're thinking. Nerves may cripple you to start with, but over time and with the help of your friends and family, you'll get the hang of it..

But this is just the beginning. Taking care of a wee, defenceless baby is tough enough, but this is just the start of a lifelong journey for mum and child. Not only will you have to deal with his or her temper tantrums and make sure he or she hasn't crawled into the middle of the road, you will also tirelessly worry about his or her mental health, being bullied and whether or not they are old enough to take on certain responsibilities. You will begin to question yourself, too. How much time should you spend with your child? When are you actually allowed to have time off? Should you feel guilty about it or is it natural for every mum to take five to enjoy some 'me' time. And then what happens when the kids get older? How much freedom do we give them? How protective should we be? Or should we let them make their own mistakes? Being a mum isn't easy. And there is no big book of how to be the best mum. So, for now, let's see how our favourite Loose Women have dealt with being mums and the hurdles they have had to jump and discover what we can learn from them.

STARTING OUT

DOES PARENTING COME NATURALLY?

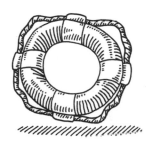

There's an expectation that as soon as the baby is born a bond will be forged between you straight away, and you'll instinctively know what to do. But that's not always the case. Every new mum experiences those first few weeks differently, and at times it can feel overwhelming.

Some women, like Gloria, believe that women 'are born nurturers' who naturally take to the role, although she concedes that being a new mum isn't easy. 'Yes, of course it is scary,' she says. 'The first time you bath your baby, he or she is all slippery with soap, and the realisation sets in that you are fully responsible for this gorgeous baby. However, I think the majority of women dream about the day they will give birth.'

But then there are women like Nadia who says she didn't have a clue about how to be a mum.

'When I had children, I thought it would all come to me naturally and I'd be a brilliant parent, but actually I was a far worse parent than I ever thought I was going to be,' Nadia confesses. 'I struggled with a lot of things. I thought I was going to be an earth mother! I thought I was going to be brilliant, but I found it *really* hard – I was quite rubbish. I was like a shaking-jelly wreck not knowing what to do.'

But instead of whipping herself into a panicky frenzy and worrying about it all on her own, she turned to the people who knew her best – her family.

'I did reach out to people and get help and advice,' she says. 'Every time I needed to ask questions, it was always to my friends or my sister, or to my mum that I turned to and who all proved to be a brilliant support network. I've got a loving husband too, but to be honest men don't know the answer to a lot of the questions I was asking. I think it's important to have a support network when you're a new parent. There's still a lot of shame attached to people saying they're struggling with being a parent, but people shouldn't be ashamed to ask for help.'

Kaye explains that because she hadn't grown up with dreams of being a blushing bride in white or starting a family, it was only later when she had settled down with partner Ian that children became a conversation.

'It wasn't that I wasn't maternal, but I had never felt the urge to be a parent. But then at 35 I had the urge and I was 36 when I had Charly,' Kaye recalls. 'And it was big change for me. When you have had a good chunk of your adult life doing as you please, the idea of looking after another person is quite terrifying. I was lucky enough to have a good job and a good income and a nice relationship, then to suddenly put your own needs and desires to one side and to elevate this little thing to centre stage was difficult.'

Kaye says that although she was confident in many of aspects her life, becoming a mum left her feeling out of her depth.

'I found it difficult,' she confesses. 'Initially I was a basket case because I felt like I lost control. I remember when my daughter had bad colic during the first three months – she was screaming at 3pm in the afternoon and would cry that high-pitched cry until 10 at night. I came to dread that. I would hear the theme of *Corrie* and all I wanted to do was sit down with a glass of wine and watch it. But I had this little baby who I had to walk around the garden. It reminded me that I was no longer first and I will admit I struggled with that a little bit.'

Kaye thinks that it took a few months for it all to click into place, and for her to feel she had really bonded with her daughter – but even that felt a little intimidating. 'She was about four months old, and we were on holiday somewhere and she properly giggled for the first time at something. It was that fit of uncontrollable giggles that a baby will have that tends to go viral on social media. It was that moment that I realised it was a relationship and not just my duty to look after this defenceless creature. And that scared me. I knew I loved this child, but the idea of the responsibility of looking after a child was overwhelming.'

Gloria gave birth to Caron, her first child, unexpectedly early during a trip to London. She and Don were in the middle of watching *Oliver!* in the West End when suddenly her waters broke and all hell let loose as she was raced across London in an ambulance to give birth. It meant that she went through the delivery without her mum or family by her side. 'I'd always expected that my mum would be around when I had my first baby and so I really, really missed her,' she remembers. At the same time, the experience of becoming a parent gave her a deeper understanding of her mother. 'The minute I saw Caron I suddenly realised all the angst that my parents put into our upbringing and why they didn't let you do certain things. I realised in that moment that I was responsible for this treasure. And what a treasure she turned out to be.'

Meanwhile, Saira admits she was at a loss when she first became a mum. "When I had Zac, Steve and I were in London away from our family and friends. And while having a baby was joyous, it was also scary. I had always thought of myself as a strong and independent woman. But this was the first time that I thought I had no idea what I was doing. As a business person I have always had a plan, and when things don't go your way there are solutions. But with a baby you are out of control. Luckily, my mum helped out – she was a godsend.'

IS SOLO PARENTING THE FUTURE?

Some of us remember a time when being a single mum or dad was frowned upon. Nonsense, right? After all, how many amazing single parents do you know who have brought up well-behaved and well-rounded young men and women? Thankfully, we are now living in an age in which some women who haven't found a partner with whom they want to settle down are fast forwarding to having a baby.

Jane, a confident and determined career woman, says she is right behind women taking control of their parental destiny and even admits that had she not been in a relationship herself by a certain age, she might have taken matters into her own hands.

'I absolutely would have had a child on my own,' she states. 'A lot of women are looking for Mr Right and they want to have a baby within the scenario of being in a committed relationship, but that doesn't always happen any more. Your biological clock thinks, "Well, I'm desperate to have a child and I don't have a partner so I'm going to go a clinic".'

Although now happily married to PR guru Gary, Jane remembers a time just after having her first daughter when she found herself back on the dating scene, now with a baby in tow. 'I had Ellie when I was 31 and in a relationship. Then that ended so I had a period of time when I was a single mum,' she recalls.

Although she had no partner to rely on, she was never far away from family. 'I was lucky because my mum lived literally on the next road. So I had this fantastic support network and I never really felt like a single parent in the same way that some people might.'

Nadia says she has noticed that more women are starting their families later in life and, in a number of cases, on their own. However, she points out that even though these older mums may have more control over their lives and may continue with work until they are in their 40s, their bodies are still biologically designed to have kids at an early age.

'Because life around us has changed so much and as women we are much more empowered than we ever were, we forget that our bodies haven't changed,' she says. 'Biologically, we are still made to have children at a much younger age than many of us are even starting. It's so easy for it to pass us by and women have to be careful.'

Now in her mid-fifties, Jane says her views on starting a family have most definitely changed over the years, influenced by shifting attitudes in society. She says she now gives her older daughter different advice than she used to.

'I've always told Ellie, "Your twenties are for being selfish, and then you mustn't even think about having children until you're in your thirties!"' Jane says. 'But now she's in her late twenties and I'm telling her, "I've had a change of heart!". Me and Nadia both had our second children naturally at the grand old age of 42. Statistically, we are literally a miracle!' Jane doesn't want her daughters to leave it too late as she knows how lucky she was to get pregnant later in life.

ON STRUGGLING TO BECOME A MUM

While studies have shown that, in general, women's fertility begins to decline in their thirties, there are those who find it particularly difficult to conceive. Saira is one of these women. When she married her husband Steve, she had no question in her head that they would start a family straight away. But nature had other plans. In spite of her numerous attempts to fall pregnant, it just didn't seem to happen. For a while, Saira just couldn't understand why she wasn't able to get pregnant because she thought her body was, she would admit, in pristine condition for producing offspring.

'At first I thought, "Well, I'm healthy, I'm a good weight, I keep fit, I don't drink, I don't smoke, I've never done drugs, I don't even take painkillers. So why isn't it happening?"' She says, 'It was hard for me to get my head around because it seemed there was no reason why I shouldn't be getting pregnant.'

After two years of trying, Saira and Steve decided to seek medical advice and underwent a series of tests to determine what the problem was. Doctors told her that she had endometriosis, a condition where tissue similar to the lining of the womb starts to grow in other places, such as the ovaries and fallopian tubes. The diagnosis came as 'a real shock' to Saira but on the other hand also offered her 'a sense of relief' as now she knew why falling pregnant had been proving to be so difficult. So Saira and Steve tried IVF and thankfully it worked. However, the birth wasn't easy as Saira was forced to undergo an emergency caesarean after a long and painful labour, but it resulted in the birth of their beautiful son Zac.

Looking back at that arduous experience, Saira says that the one thing comes to mind that fills her warmth was the enduring support of her beloved husband. 'Steve was amazing. When I had my caesarean with Zac, I was in hospital for three days and I genuinely couldn't move. Steve saw me in my worst condition, my legs were all bandaged up to prevent clotting. I looked like the Mummy in bed! But he was amazing. He had to help me to the loo and everything, it was terrible. And I had to have these shields attached to help Zac latch on when I was breastfeeding, and Steve had to boil them up to sterilise them every day. He deserves an MBE!'

In spite of the pain that came with the first pregnancy, Saira and Steve were keen to add to their brood. But no sooner had they started trying again for a baby than it became clear that falling pregnant still wouldn't be easy. Again they turned to IVF. But this time it wasn't so easy. 'With IVF you are told not to build up your hopes,' Saira reminisces. 'But because the first one worked I thought this would be as easy. But when it didn't happen, I was disappointed but not heartbroken because we already had another plan and had started thinking about adoption.'

And so Saira decided to travel to Pakistan – with a documentary crew in tow – in the hope of adopting a baby. The trip to the country would not only change their lives but also the life of a baby less than a week old.

'Six days after we arrived in Pakistan, I got a phone call from an orphanage telling us that they had a baby who had just been found abandoned that week,' she recalls. 'From their initial analysis, the little girl was just four days old and was very frail. So I suggested to the director of the documentary, "Look, you may want to turn your cameras off, because this is very touch and go." Amara, the little girl, was then rushed into intensive care where she was given urgent medical attention. I felt helpless.'

Saira was on tenterhooks for the next seven days, waiting anxiously to find out what the outcome for little Amara would be. In spite of their brief encounter and the lack of information available about the little girl's background, Saira felt as though she had bonded with Amara deeply and was determined to take her home to meet her new daddy. Steve had stayed in the UK with their son Zac, who was two years old at the time, and was desperately waiting for news. Saira recalls, 'I told the staff, "This baby is mine and whatever happens to her I'm taking her back to the UK."'

Amara was finally ready to meet the rest of her new family in the UK. Back home, Steve and Saira were advised to undergo a parenting course. While she initially thought it unnecessary – after all she'd already successfully brought up one well-rounded young child – she admits that she did learn a few new things along the way.

'For one, it taught me how to communicate with my child and actually make time to listen,' she says. 'My childhood was quite traumatic in parts and I found as a mother I was beginning to repeat the same parenting skills with my children. It was only when I went on that parenting course that I realised that my mum and dad hadn't got it right. I actually now welcome help for me as a parent, so that I can be a better parent to my child.'

From the outset, Saira was encouraged by social workers and the charity that set up the adoption to be transparent at all times with Amara about where she had come from and tell her that she had been adopted.

'This was something to be celebrated,' she says. 'I wanted her to know that she was no different to anybody else. I wanted her to know that I was her mummy and that she had another tummy mummy who had brought her into the world. Now if the subject of her adoption comes up in conversation Amara knows straight away that she didn't come out of my tummy but that I am her mummy.'

Even though it's unlikely that they will ever meet Amara's natural mum, Saira says she often sends out a mental message to the 'tummy mummy' to say thank you for everything that she's done and to assure her that Amara is being well looked after.

LOOSE LESSONS

- If you don't find being a mum easy, don't worry, this is normal. Lots of women feel out of their depth during the early days.

- When you feel like you don't know what you're doing, ask a friend, family member or your other half – you are not alone.

- If you're struggling to get pregnant, there are many ways you can fulfil your dream. You can try IVF, adoption, fostering... There are lots of options so start researching.

LIFE AFTER BIRTH

DOES YOUR RELATIONSHIP CHANGE AFTER THE BABY IS BORN?

 When the new little one starts bawling at 2am, neither parent is likely to be getting much sleep as they try to navigate this new, scary world of parenthood. After the physical impact of the birth, along with the demands of breastfeeding, some women can feel at this time that their body is not their own. So it comes as no surprise that sometimes couples drift apart during this new stage of their relationship...

Gloria remembers that the first few months after her daughter Caron was born were very tough on her relationship with her husband Don. It wasn't long before she started to feel resentment because he didn't have to work as hard as she did for their newborn.

'A lot of the images we see today of motherhood are about being perfect and getting back your figure, but the ripple effect is quite something,' she recalls. 'I breastfed Caron for nine months and the pressure was definitely on to give your baby the best milk. But a kind of resentment built up. My first husband Don snored a lot, and it's not like he could have breastfed the baby instead. I remember being quite resentful and thinking it was all right for him because he could snore through it. I was exhausted and still had to do it. I used to read really racy novels to get me through the night – *Fifty Shades of Grey* has nothing on me!'

Like Gloria, Jane explains that when she had her first child, her relationship with her then partner changed dramatically because resentment began to build. 'Ellie's dad and I were in our twenties when we met and we were clubbing and pubbing and doing all the things young couples do,' she explains. 'Then three years in, we decided to have a baby. Once Ellie was born, my perception of my boyfriend completely changed. I was the one who changed and suddenly felt more responsible. I was working full time, as I thought I needed to start earning money to pay for our flat and the bills. But he stayed the same as he was before Ellie had come along and that made me mad.'

And this was the wake-up call Jane needed. 'It's at times like that when you suddenly look at a man and ask, "How are you going to provide?" How will you meet me halfway with everything?" That's really what split up our relationship. But he's a lovely guy and we're still friends.'

Nadia, meanwhile, tells a different story. She and husband Mark had only been together three months before she discovered she was pregnant. But when the baby finally arrived Nadia suffered the shocking realisation that both their lives were about to change beyond recognition.

'Before we got pregnant, Mark and I loved going out and pubbing a lot. And then when Maddie came along, I thought all of a sudden, "I can't go to the pub any more.' I remember a week after the baby was born urging Mark to "go to Soho, go out". But the minute he went out the door, I was left with this baby on my breast just wanting stuff, crying my eyes out that I couldn't go to the pub too. But we had to grow up. We worked our way through it. But I'm not going to sugarcoat it. It was so, so difficult for us to start with. And I think I was a little traumatised by the massive change in my life; that I didn't know how to be me. Nor did I know what exactly Mark and I were, probably because we'd be together just four months and we weren't really ready to work out what we wanted from our lives.'

Coleen says that giving birth to her first baby, Shane Jr, didn't change her relationship with her husband, but actually changed the way she viewed herself. 'When my baby came out, rather than thinking of what my husband thought, I just applauded *me*,' she says, looking back with pride. 'I just went, "Oh my God, I'm a warrior." I was so proud of myself. Up until having the first one, I used to faint at the thought of going to the dentist and here I was, pushing this baby out. I didn't care what Shane thought, I just thought, "I'm great! I'm so much better than you!" He was the kind of guy who'd faint if he stubbed his toe and I'd just produced a baby.'

Saira, on the other hand, says that her relationship with Steve changed the minute they decided it was the time in their lives to start a family. 'The moment we started planning and were told we had to have IVF, our relationship changed. Steve was at every scan, every blood test. He was there all the way through. For me, we became a unit. When you get married, you are together, but planning and starting a family is a strong bond for life. I mean, if we didn't have children and we had a row there would have been less of a reason to try to work it out.'

IS THERE A PRESSURE TO BREASTFEED YOUR KIDS?

A lot of women are led to believe that when it comes to feeding their newborns, it's as easy as pie. While some mothers and babies do happily take to the process like a duck to water, some find it very hard indeed. Some even feel unsure about what they have to do in the first place, while others can find the entire procedure painful and unpleasant.

Nadia, for one, is not shy to admit that when she was a new mum she was pretty clueless. Not only did she feel too awkward to feed her little one in public, fearful of judgement from those around her, she also felt unsure when it came to technique.

'I was embarrassed, ashamed and forced to hide away when I was breastfeeding, at a time when I was also feeling very vulnerable, guilty and like a terrible mother,' she recalls. 'And I didn't feel like I was supported by anyone around me. The biggest problem in society for me is that we, the UK, are one of the few countries where we don't actually see anyone breastfeeding in public, which I am happy to say is definitely changing.'

Nadia was so anxious about the process of breastfeeding that she eventually decided to seek professional advice to ease her worries. 'I went to a four-hour lesson about how to breastfeed a baby because I had never seen it being done before and I have to say it helped a great deal,' she explains. 'In other cultures, kids see women breastfeeding all the time and they are subliminally being taught how to breastfeed. I have to admit I had a terrible experience, but I persevered and persevered and I'm glad I did. We women make this incredible thing that is breastmilk and you can burn 500 calories doing it. Result!'

But that doesn't mean that all women must do it, and not all women are physically able to do it. A lot of new mums experience some problems when it comes to doing what nature suggests they should be in tune with. Coleen, who has had breastfeeding issues, says she thinks it's unfair that all women should be expected to take to breastfeeding easily and certainly shouldn't be made to feel guilty about it if they don't.

'I didn't breastfeed my boys because I was still working and I was young and didn't have the inclination,' she reminisces. 'I had the biggest boobs in school at 13 and everyone would say to me "you're going to be a great mum with those" but they were useless. They were rubbish!'

However, when she fell pregnant with Ciara, she decided that as this was most likely her last pregnancy, she would give breastfeeding one last try.

'I'd watched my sister Bernie breastfeed Erin and they loved it,' she remembers. 'Bernie really enjoyed it, while Erin took to it really easily. Ray also really wanted me to breastfeed so I thought, why not try again?'

Only the experience wasn't good for Coleen. 'It was absolutely

Nadia at the age of 21.

When Nadia was pregnant with her second daughter, Kiki.

Nadia and Mark with their daughters, Maddie and Kiki.

Nadia on holiday in Spain in 2019 with her dad, Nadim, and her mum, Roberta.

Seven-year-old Coleen with her parents, Tommy and Maureen,
in 1972. This was the day of Coleen's holy communion.

The Nolan sisters in 1975 (*from left to right:* Maureen, Linda, Anne, Denise,
Bernie, with Coleen, aged 10, front and centre).

Coleen and first husband, Shane Richie, on their wedding day in 1990.

Coleen with her three children: Jake, Ciara and Shane Jr.

Coleen dressed as Wonder Woman on *Loose Women*, one of the many fancy dress outfits that she has sported on the show!

Kaye as a baby, with her brother Eric.

Kaye, aged 16, in a hockey team photo from her final
year of school. Kaye went to Grangemouth High
School for the majority of her time but attended
Saint George's in Edinburgh for a single year.

This is a publicity photograph from Kaye's first job after university.
She was a trainee journalist with Central Television in Birmingham.

Kaye with the great love of
her life, her dog Bea.

In October 2016, Jasper Conran made Janet a special dress out of English silk to wear when she went to Buckingham Palace to receive her CBE (for services to broadcasting and journalism). Janet took three special girlfriends as her guests.

Janet eating fish and chips in Margate, September 2018, with Badger the Border terrier. Notice how the greedy blighter is licking his lips... It's pouring with rain, but, of course, that doesn't put Janet off.

Janet, in 2017, at her friend's house in Bridgehampton, USA, getting ready for Halloween. She found that a giant pumpkin makes a good seat!

Janet was in Northern New South Wales, Australia, in 2016. Janet wears her antlers on Christmas Day, no matter where in the world she is.

August 2016, when Janet was fishing off Eilean Shona on the west coast of Scotland. Janet was having an early 70th birthday celebration at a big house with her friends. She caught pollack and a lot of mackerel.

horrendous,' she concedes. 'Ciara was constantly on there but still crying. It made me kind of not want to bond with her a bit to start with, and I felt bad about that and that I was in some way a rubbish mum.'

Feeling low, Coleen carried on trying, encouraged by those around her that Ciara would eventually take to her breast. Sadly, it didn't happen.

'I had midwives saying it would be fine, who encouraged me to keep going,' she says. 'But I was in agony and she wasn't feeding properly. It was the most horrendous five weeks of my life. But I carried on regardless, because every time she cried, I had to try and feed her. But it got to the point when I would get scared if she'd stir in her cot because I knew I would have to feed her and that it would be painful and she still wouldn't be happy.'

If the lack of mother–daughter connection wasn't bad enough to contend with, Coleen was shy about feeding Ciara around other people. 'Fair play to all those mums out there who can do it,' she smiles. 'But I'm quite shy, so even in my own house I'd go and sit upstairs to do it.'

Coleen says it was after about six weeks of trying to ween Ciara on to her breast that she knew the time had come to give in. 'There was this one night Ray found me in the kitchen with Ciara on my breast,' she says, 'and I was just sobbing my heart out. For me it just hadn't worked. I couldn't do it. It just didn't happen naturally. And I felt bad. I felt like I wasn't a good mum.'

Now, however, Coleen can look back at that time more positively. 'I realise it's no one's fault if baby and mother don't immediately connect. There is such a pressure to breastfeed; you can't help but feel like you're not as good as other mums if there are problems. But I don't think anyone should be made to feel like that.'

Jane also endured a pretty rough time when it came to nursing her first daughter. In fact, after a terrible first experience, she knew exactly what to do with her next baby!

'I really felt the pressure to breastfeed my first baby, but I gave up after a couple of weeks because I was just in agony,' she says matter-of-factly. 'By the time I had my second baby, I told them: "Don't even bother, I'm not doing it!" I didn't feel guilty about it. It was just the way it was.'

Gloria breastfed when she was still singing on TV and appearing in live shows, and she soon discovered a downside – that the milk would leak all over her best frocks!

Saira remembers that breastfeeding wasn't the best experience, but felt like she was letting herself down if she didn't do it. 'I had read about breastfeeding, had done all the research and thought it would be all fine. But when it came to it, Zac didn't latch on,' she recalls. 'I was determined to do it, but it was out of my control. Then my best friend Joanna, who had had kids a few years before, came to see me and showed me a contraption called a nipple shield, and it totally changed the way I breastfed. I was so glad as I found it a great way of bonding with my child.'

However, Saira understands now that in spite of being told 'breast is best', there are other methods and that no woman should feel a failure as a mum. 'If a woman is struggling, I'd assure her that it's not for everyone. It doesn't spoil you child's start in life if he or she has to have a bottle – and that's important to remember.'

Those wanting more information or advice on breastfeeding should talk to their health visitor or contact their GP in the first instance.

IS IT POSSIBLE TO LOVE YOUR CHILDREN EQUALLY?

Surely no mum can love one child more than the other? We convince ourselves that we love our kids unconditionally, and so if sometimes we feel more drawn to one over the other it feels like a terrible thing to admit. When they become pregnant with their second child, lots of women wonder if they will experience the same love for the new baby as they did with the first, and worry about how their relationship with their older child will change. Well, don't panic if you have experienced these troubling thoughts, you are not the only one, as the Loose Women reveal...

Kaye explains that when she was pregnant with her second child, Bonnie, she was nervous about how she would feel about her, about the new baby due to burst into her life. 'There was a real period of time when I thought, "Oh no, I'm never going to be able to love the second one as much as I love the first one,"' she says. 'It felt like a betrayal and I was looking at the first one and thinking, "I'm sorry." I really did feel as if I was doing something treacherous and it really worried me.'

Nadia agrees that while she was pregnant with Kiki she too felt as though she was being deceitful to firstborn Maddie.

'I felt like I was about to be unfaithful,' she laughs about it now. 'That's the only way I can explain it. I remember I kept grabbing hold of Maddie and saying, "I love you, I love you." I was obsessed with the fact that this new baby was going to arrive and that she would feel like I'd dumped her.'

Nadia admits that the feelings became intense and that she felt uncomfortable, believing that she was the only mum in the world thinking those odd thoughts.

'It was scary,' she says. 'I felt so bad to even have the thought in my head. But then when you start talking about it with other women you soon realise that everyone feels the same.'

Once Kiki was born, however, all of Nadia's fears disappeared. 'People around me kept telling me that your love doesn't divide when you have another child, it multiplies,' she says. 'I thought that couldn't be true. But you know what? It does, you just get double the love, it just increases twofold.'

Kaye too says that she was pleased to discover that she loved her two girls equally, even though both girls were so very different from each other. 'One of them I feel is a kind of mini me; I can see what's going through her head and it's a strange experience – it feels like me,' she says. 'But the other one, I do not understand her at all! In spite of that, I love them both dearly, exactly the same.'

Gloria says when she had her children she always knew she'd love them equally no matter what. 'I can honestly say that I've always tried to treat my children the same and I could never say that I loved this one over that one. But there were things at certain times that bonded me closer to one over the other. For example, with Caron, when she got married and started having babies, as two women we automatically had this marvellous layer of jointness. And then Caron would come down at weekends to see me at my home in Sevenoaks and she would ring up her brothers to make sure they would be there too.'

'If somebody asked "which of your children are you proudest of?" I would say I'm really, really proud of all my children because they are hard workers who have never sponged off anybody. They're genuinely good people. And as I see them getting older I can see what fine people they have grown into. You know you'll always love your children. You don't always like them necessarily, because of certain issues or behaviour. But generally I like my children and I enjoy spending time with them enormously. They provide some of the best fun I have ever had. The best nights for me are when my children and my grandchildren are around, all round the table. I love it. It is joyful and magic.'

DO WE STILL TREAT BOYS AND GIRLS DIFFERENTLY?

We've come a long way since boys wore blue and girls looked pretty in pink, and men aspired to be leaders at work while their wives looked after the house. Times have changed, and these days men happily use cosmetic products without raising their mates' plucked eyebrows, women wear trousers and do DIY, dads stay at home to look after the kids while mums fight fires. It's *almost* like we're living in a modern, equal world...

However, when it comes to expressing emotions, there's still a massive division between the sexes. Men still find it hard to talk about their sensitive issues, not helped by outdated views instilled in them from childhood, such as being told to 'man up' and get on with it. And that can be ultimately catastrophic.

According to the Samaritans, 84 men a week take their own lives and suicide is ranked as the biggest killer of men under the age of 45. And yet, some men are still bringing up their sons to encourage them to show no emotion in public, a practice that our Loose Ladies take serious issue with.

'I grew up in a generation where men said things like "man up" and nobody batted an eyelid,' Saira rages. 'I think comments like that are sexist. I feel like men have been brainwashed into thinking that's what men are supposed to be like, "Have a stiff upper lip, don't cry", or if it's a girl then you have to be really soft with her.'

Saira says she treats her children equally and embraces the fact that her son shows a more emotional nature and therefore treats him accordingly. 'I come from a culture where boys were treated differently from girls,' she explains. 'There's an instinct in me that boys and girls are equal. Equality is important to me. However, I think because Amara was adopted I feel a vulnerability towards her because of the way she came into our lives.'

In spite of her not raising her children any differently from each other, she says she has noticed over time that Amara is a lot more resilient than her son, whom she describes as super sensitive.

'Someone at school said to Amara one day, "She's not your real mum, your real mum didn't want you." She said to the girl, "You don't know what you're talking about" and walked off. But when Zac heard he started crying and asked why people are so cruel. Emotionally she is stronger than him. My son is a cuddler and I give him space to cry because I came from a culture where men didn't open up, which often resulted in self-destruction. Talking about stuff is so important. I let my daughter see my son cry. She looks after him all the time.'

Coleen says she understands the way some men have been conditioned to ignore or play down their feelings, yet she admits that she did sometimes treat her boys Shane Jr and Jake differently from her daughter Ciara as they were growing up. 'I would never ever say to a boy "man up and don't cry",' she says. 'I always try to treat my kids exactly the same. But when they were little, whenever people would play really rough with the boys – wrestling and throwing them around – I'd think they were both loving it. However, when I'd see someone doing it with Ciara, a part of me instinctively would think, "Don't be so rough with her!" Don't get me wrong, it wasn't me saying she was weaker than the boys. It was just an instinctive thing.'

However, now that Shane Jr and Jake have grown up into strapping young men and moved away from home, she is concerned that they might not be as open talking about deep-rooted issues as they might be.

'When women go out we discuss absolutely everything,' she says. 'We have a laugh but we always end up talking about problems regarding relationships or children. But men say they just don't do that. And that worries me, especially as my boys get older. They are both completely and utterly different. Jake is very open with his emotions, good or bad, and we can sit up until four in the morning discussing everything. Shane Jr is a typical boy; when I know he's down about something, he'll just say, "I'm fine". He's the one who worries me most. I can't force him to talk to me. He always says, "Mum, don't worry about me I am not going to do something stupid." But you do worry because you think, just open up to me!'

Like Coleen, Gloria has always encouraged her boys Michael and Paul to be as open as possible. 'I've always wanted them to know that they could talk to me about anything. No matter what's bothering them, I tell them to just let me know,' she says.

However, she admits that without meaning to she did relate

to daughter Caron in a different way to her sons. 'I think that you automatically treat them a little bit differently,' she confesses. 'You would like to think that your parenting values are the same, but girls are so different from boys. I think you psychologically want to protect the girl more because she appears to be more vulnerable. But I wouldn't say that I nurtured Caron more than Paul and Michael. Still to this day – although we've sadly lost Caron – Michael and Paul are two of the most important people in my life and we talk on the phone every day, which some people find a bit odd. But we always have stuff to catch up on. And no Irish mother wants her child further than around the corner.'

TALKING TO KIDS ABOUT PUBERTY

As many of us will have experienced, one of the most difficult times in a child's life is when they start puberty. Not only do they get grumpy, grow hair and develop spots, there then comes the moment when parents have to do 'the chat'. Some parents find it understandably awkward to talk to their youngsters about the birds and the bees, while for others – like Nadia – it's a piece of cake to get chatty about what goes in where...

'I've been talking to the kids about it since they were babies,' she says. 'If you start the conversation from a young age, you never have to endure that really embarrassing moment when you sit down and say, "Right now, let's have THE conversation."'

Nadia says that nothing is off limits in the conversations she has with her two daughters at home. 'Periods, sex, boys... are topics that are never taboo in my house,' she says proudly. 'For example, when Maddie was tiny and I was still breastfeeding, I couldn't leave her so I used to take her to the loo with me and she'd see the sanitary towels and tampons. Eventually she asked what they were, so I told her. Then one day, when I was in the bath and she was on the loo, she announced matter-of-factly: "Oh, mum, I've started my periods."'

As a result of this refreshingly open chat, Nadia is pleased to see that her other daughter feels relaxed enough to calmly talk about the changes taking place in her body. 'Kiki-Bee is probably learning things much faster because there are so many conversations going on around her. I think having an older sister is an advantage for her in that way,' she says. 'I try to show my girls that they don't have to feel uncomfortable about anything to do with their bodies. When we went for a bra fitting, Maddie said: "Oh no, I hope there's no one there to measure me. I don't want to get my boobs out." But I explained that they can measure her over the top of the bra and that she really doesn't need to feel self-conscious.'

Nadia was brought up in a strict household, but her mum encouraged open conversation about women's issues. However, Nadia says that her mum didn't really deal with her daughter's body insecurities. 'My mum was quite open about periods but I never really spoke to her about body image because in my house it was all very, "Don't be silly, you're lovely." But it's not silly, because even if you tell your daughter she is the most beautiful person in the world, it doesn't necessarily mean anything to her. That means nothing at all if you're 13 and you've got spots or you don't like your tummy. As mums, we have to give teens the space to have a moan about things like that and not dismiss their feelings.'

But Nadia is not the only one to always listen to Maddie and Kiki. Their dad Mark has also proved to be a very open and understanding father. 'Mark is so hands-on. The girls talk to him about anything,' Nadia explains. 'We were at the cinema this one time and Maddie whispered as we queued for our tickets, "Mum, I've just come on my period." Mark was at the back of the queue and there is no way he could have heard us, yet when I mouthed to him that he needed to go to the chemist, he just knew why straight away. Minutes later he was back with a carrier bag with every kind of sanitary product you could find.'

ARE YOU A SELFISH PARENT?

Sometimes just cooking and cleaning for your kids, while trying to nurture them *and* keep them safe *and* make sure they get to school on time, feels like a Herculean task. So what happens when – once all the chores are finally done, and you're slumped exhausted on the sofa – your son or daughter chooses that moment to beg you to play a game with them, or help them paint a picture. When you've had very little time for yourself, it's understandable if you're not dying to spend your quality time and rare 'me moments' pretending to be the big, bad ogre terrorising your kid's cuddly toys. Then, more often than not, a wave of guilt for not wanting to join in washes over you...

But wait – sometimes it's actually OK to be a little bit selfish, otherwise you're likely to send yourself around the bend.

'Playing with your kids is boring,' Coleen declares, matter-of-factly. 'It's lovely for ten minutes, but then an hour later, you're still there and they're going, "Again, again!" There's only so many times you can build blocks to watch them hilariously knock them down.'

It wasn't just silly games that tried Coleen's patience – her daughter's lack of attention to detail almost sent over her over the edge!

'When Ciara was younger, she'd ask me to sit and do colouring in with her, but she'd ruin it by going over the lines and that would annoy me!' she recalls. 'So I'd play with them for a little bit and then do something else. I didn't feel guilty or anything. I mean, I gave birth to her – was that not enough?! What more does she want?!'

Nadia reckons that all parents are selfish to a degree and would rather be sat down in front of the telly than cross-legged on the floor pretending to be excited about a Barbie doll and a toy dinosaur.

'Aren't we all a bit selfish?' she asks. 'I mean, I can remember so many occasions when I was reading a story or playing with the kids' toys and I wished I was somewhere else. Probably downstairs, having a drink, having a bag of crisps. I remember when they used to ask me to play Barbies and I used to sometimes play in the most boring way I possibly could so that I could get back to doing whatever it was that I was doing. Then they'd be like, "Mum, you're rubbish" and I'd be like, "OK! See you later!"'

Nadia decided that when she became a mum she would raise her kids in a more liberal way than her own mum had. 'I told myself I was going be the complete antithesis of my mum because she was the kind of parent who would make you sit at the table until you ate what you didn't like,' she says. 'I remember sitting there with tears running down my face saying to myself, "I promise I will never a mummy like this."'

However, Nadia does confess that her experience with her daughters has shown that perhaps there was something in her mum's stricter methods. 'Now I'm paying the price for being a relaxed parent because my girls won't eat anything!' she laughs. 'They are so fussy, so actually my mum was – dare I say – right and I was, er, wrong. My mum was really strict with bedtimes and I used to go to bed and go, "I hate my mum, I'm in bed, I'm alive, I don't want to be in bed" so I'm not going be so strict with bedtimes, I regret it. She did those things for a reason. I'm a bit too hippy.'

While Nadia's mum might not have been as playful as others, Nadia acknowledges that she did give her the necessary attention and support when it came to more important things in Nadia's life. 'The thing that my mum always said, no matter what hair-brained scheme I came up with, no matter what dream I had, was, "That's great, do it!"'

Kaye says she was OK that her mum wasn't a playful type. 'I had a fabulous relationship with my mum, but if I ever said, "Mum, come and play in the garden," she'd look at me as if I'd grown horns,' she laughs. 'She just didn't do that. She had other things to do, she was working full time. I didn't expect it, and I didn't really want it to be honest. I wanted to be in the park; I wanted to be having fun with my pals. If there was a kid in the park playing with their mum, I probably would have thought they were really quite sad.'

As opposed to being put off by it, Kaye says she was inspired by her mum's style of parenting and took it on when it came to bringing up her own kids. 'I am almost the same parent my mum was,' she says proudly. 'When I reflect on it, I am very, very similar. I guess I have changed a little bit, but that's due mainly to social pressure. I think my mum got it right. I loved the independence. I absolutely knew that she was rock solid and that if I needed her she was there and she wasn't strict at all – I could get round her dead easy – but I had the independence, you know. I was off doing my own thing, which I loved.'

HOW HARD IS IT TO BE A MUM AND HAVE A CAREER?

If you've ever balanced life as a mum with a career you'll know it's not easy. Do women need to be realistic and rethink their attitudes to their careers once they have welcomed a little one into the world, or should women be given more help to get back to work after taking time out to have children?

Back in 2015, Vivienne Durham, then headmistress of independent Francis Holland School, Regent's Park, made headlines when she said that girls were being lied to when they were told there was no glass ceiling at work. She thinks that ultimately women have to make a choice about starting a family or embarking on a successful career. 'We all have a biological calendar and you have to make decisions about your entire working life, which probably goes up to about 77 now,' she was quoted as saying. 'But you have to make decisions about 40 per cent of your life early on. Some... will juggle and combine everything and that will be the future for lots of women. I certainly want women to have that choice.'

But is this really the case? Should women have to choose between family and work? Can't women have babies and still excel in business? Or should girls be warned they have to choose?

Jane says she understands that women have difficult choices to make as they get older, and that when they are choosing a career path they have to bear in mind the effect on their career if they decide to have children.

Jane says, 'If you had a daughter who said she wanted to be a surgeon, every mum would be thrilled. But when that young woman wants to have children of her own, her job will be affected because she might struggle to be there at 7pm to do that operation.'

Jane says that she meets so many women her age who have taken time out from the rat race to bring up a child and not gone back to the same role. 'I see women at the school gates who were high flyers, who stepped away to have children; they stop and can't get back in again. And then they do entrepreneurial stuff, which is great. I think girls should just be realistic and know that sometimes things have to give.'

Gloria says that it is natural to feel bad if you are out at work, 'All mothers feel guilty up to a point, especially if the kids are feeling poorly,' she says. However, she says that when she was starting out in her dream career as a broadcaster, she never let having a baby slow her down. Looking back, she says, it was crazy. 'I went back to work two weeks after Michael was born,' she admits. 'I've always loved working, still love work and I always have a zest for it. Ever since I was seven years old I was out singing with my dad and it made me very independent. So when it came to returning to work I was determined to do it and to manage to fit it in because I was starting to carve out a career as a broadcaster.'

Luckily, Gloria explains, she had family on hand to help her look after the kids. 'It fitted in because my sister was living nearby. When Caron was very young, I'd leave her with her for a day. I was freelance back then, so I was pottering all over the place, recording material. But while I enjoyed being busy, I was a mum first and foremost. Later, I would try really hard to make work fit around my family life so I could drop the children off at school in the morning and pick them up in the afternoon.'

When Gloria started broadcasting in 1969 it was a time of bombs, bullets and barricades. Even though she would occasionally be called away from the kids to do reports from the dangerous streets of Belfast during the days of the political troubles in Northern Ireland, she appreciates that her career offered her children experiences they might not have had otherwise. 'There were a lot of advantages, like when I took them with me to the zoo, where a polar bear had given birth to a cub. They experienced things they might not have. Before she ever presented it, Caron was mad about *Blue Peter*, but because I was known in Northern Ireland I could bypass the circuit – for example I arranged for her to meet Lesley Judd [a *Blue Peter* presenter at the time] when she was over in Belfast. I'd like to think I was very hands-on as a parent. I kind of thought that I should expose them to everything – so I took them to the theatre, the opera and the cinema. They didn't like everything, but at least I exposed them to it!'

Saira understands that it can be hard for women to balance a career with motherhood but thinks they should be encouraged to want to achieve the most they can career-wise and be a good mum.

'I don't agree that women should plan for children and then be prepared to hit a glass ceiling,' she says defiantly. 'I don't want my daughter to worry about a glass ceiling. I saw my mum go to work in a factory, come home then cook and clean. She was a warrior.'

However, Saira views success very differently from Jane, who thinks that the glass ceiling exists for women in industries like the medical, legal or business worlds who take time out to have children. For Saira, her life goal seems a lot different.

'What I learned from my mum is what does "have it all" mean? For me, that means having financial independence and the family I want, not necessarily having a high-flying job.'

That said, she believes that one day women who do work in legal and medical industries will be able to balance motherhood with a career.

'A lot of industries are old fashioned and don't offer flexibility to women,' she says. 'I'm sure, in the next ten, fifteen years, technology will allow women the career they want to pursue at their own pace and to make their own decisions.'

Coleen thinks that we as a society shouldn't make women feel guilty if they choose career over motherhood or vice versa. 'I will always support my daughter in whatever she wants to do in the future,' Coleen says. 'The main thing for women is to stop feeling guilty about everything we do. No one should be made to feel guilty if they want to be a stay-at-home mum. And no one should be made to feel guilty if they want to go work.'

LOOSE LESSONS

- Not every woman takes to breastfeeding. It can be painful and it might not be successful. Don't feel bad if you can't, just take of your child in the best way that you can and grab a bottle!

- When pregnant with baby number two, we may worry that we will love one child more than the other. Don't worry, once they are born, we love our kids equally. Whether we always like them is another matter!

- Don't feel guilty about needing your own 'me' time. It's completely normal to not want to be a mum every minute of every day.

DISCIPLINING YOUR CHILDREN

ARE WE TOO SCARED TO DISCIPLINE OUR CHILDREN?

We all know how naughty kids can be, but finding the best way to teach them right from wrong can be emotionally fraught. Not long ago, many parents would smack their kids, but these days that particular method of punishment is seriously frowned upon. Instead, parents are encouraged to talk about their child's bad behaviour and try to make them understand why what they have done is wrong. Does that really work? Or do you have to be a tough parent to show your naughty child right from wrong?

Saira says she believes that children need to be taught a lesson when they behave badly, especially if they put themselves in danger. When her son Zac was seven years old, he snuck out of the house one night to play games with a friend, which left her with no option but to give him a serious telling off.

'We disciplined him. We made sure that he absolutely knew that he had done something wrong. We told him about the dangers of what he had done and warned him of all the things that could have happened to him and that he shouldn't be doing stuff like that again.'

Saira says she is not the kind of mum to sit down and chat with her son like mates about where he had gone wrong. 'We didn't punish him mildly and say, "Let's talk about this." We told him quite blatantly, "You have done something wrong!"'

Saira admits that she was so concerned by her son's behaviour that she sought medical advice to make sure her son's actions were not the start of a new wave of bad behaviour.

'It was out of character, so we decided to go to the doctor to find out if there was a larger problem looming. We asked him, "Is this something we should worry about?" And he assured us that all was fine. He said, "Zac doesn't understand the dangers he put himself in." However, he said to us, "If you have disciplined him and he decides to go against what you've said and does it again, then there is a pattern emerging and then that could potentially be serious." So we disciplined him once and I'm glad to say Zac's never done it again.'

Saira believes that a lot of parents don't discipline their kids enough and as a result they have grown up neither respecting other people nor the law. She also thinks schools should player a bigger role in children's discipline and have the right to be harsher with their punishments. 'A lot of parents out there just don't discipline their children any more – they're too scared to say, "No, that's wrong!"' she says. 'I really think teachers should be given more powers at school to keep kids on the straight and narrow. I think that's why we're living in the world we are today!'

But what is discipline these days? What are parents allowed to do to ensure their kids learn a lesson? When Saira was younger her dad was a tough disciplinarian. 'I love my dad dearly, but he didn't know anything about discipline other than smacking,' she recalls. 'I'd get home and he'd smack my legs until they bled with a wire coat hanger. There were many occasions when I was disciplined like that. I don't blame him for doing it, but all these years on, I've had to go to therapy to understand why I'm so hard and why I get so angry. I don't discipline my kids like that because I know what it was like when I was eight years old.'

Saira's idea of discipline is very different from that of her father's. In her case, it is establishing with the child exactly who the parent is. 'I think most people connect discipline with smacking,' she explains. 'But it's not about that. It's about giving clear boundaries and saying I am the mother, you are the child. This is right. This is wrong!'

Nadia, however, approaches dealing with bad behaviour in a very new-age way and is adamant that smacking has no place in the world today. 'Whenever I see an adult smack a child it's a bigger person hitting a smaller person and it really upsets me,' she reflects. 'I wouldn't even smack my girls on the hand. I just don't like it. I don't believe in any contact. I think all smacking is physically abusive. It's just violence.'

Smacked as a child herself, she admits that she thinks she learned no lessons, but instead harboured feelings of anger and resentment instead. 'I grew up being smacked in the way seventies kids were,' she explains. 'My mum smacked me, just as she had been when she was growing up. But when she smacked me all I felt was resentment and anger toward her. And for me it just didn't work.'

Nadia thinks parents should be setting kids an example of how to live better lives instead of using outdated forms of punishment to keep them on the straight and narrow.

'I think everything we do should inspire our children, like eating well,' she says. 'I try not to swear so my children don't copy me. I want to show that when I am frustrated or angry and can't get my point across I am not going to hit someone. I am going to try a different way.'

Gloria says that when she grew up in macho Ireland her dad was the 'boss in our household' but would never hit her, while her mum would give her a whack around the legs. However, when it came to disciplining her own children she was pretty tough. 'I remember, I went ballistic with Paul when he was about 13 because he lied to me about attending a rugby game,' she recalls. 'His teacher had called home to tell me that he hadn't turned up, so when he came home I asked him how the match went. He said, "Yeah it was fine, we won." Because I knew he was lying, something in me just blew and I said to him, "You're telling me lies. You didn't even go to the match. Don't you ever do that." I was doing the dishes at the time, so I threw one of my good china cups at him, which hit the wall. Of course, he ducked and I lost a cup. I can't stand people telling lies. "You let the team down," I said, "you didn't even go to the match." You see, I was taught that you had to honour your word, which I'm proud to say still resonates with me today.'

Gloria says that when daughter Caron was battling cancer, she was impressed and inspired by the calm way Caron disciplined her kids. 'When she decided to stay on in Australia, her son Charlie, who was seven at the time, flew off into the most awful rage shouting, "You promised me we would be going back to Cornwall soon." Caron was running after him trying to placate him. And then she sat him down and said calmly, "You know, Charlie, the thing is that when you're old enough you can decide for yourself where you want to be and what you want to do, but at the minute because you're with me and you're underage, this is what I need to do for me and my health. You'll have to take my word for it that this is the best way forward." And I thought that method of negotiating definitely wasn't me. I probably would have been saying, "We're staying here because I say so!" But it did the job, so I guess in some cases it works. And I personally learned something from Caron.'

HOW CAN YOU TAME A TANTRUM CHILD?

One of the biggest challenges parents face is dealing with children who turn Tasmanian devil. It's every parent's nightmare – their child face down in the fruit and veg aisle of the supermarket, beating their fists on the floor and screaming at the top of their lungs. But how do we temper them? Shout at them? What is the best way to deal with a child when they are in full tantrum mode?

Experts say parents should always stay calm, ignore the tantrum and never beg or try to negotiate. But that is easier said than done, right? Especially when you are out in public and your child is making an unholy din.

Kaye thinks that taming a ballistic child can be one of the hardest jobs a mother can take on, as in the heat of the moment the little one is struggling with their emotions and not being particularly logical, so when 'you try to apply logic to them they just get confused'.

Nadia agrees and says that sometimes trying to reason with them can only make matters worse. 'If you try and negotiate with them and you're getting crosser, they back themselves into a corner and then they don't know how to come out of it,' she says.

Kaye says she has learned over the years from experience how to diffuse the situation. 'I have two very different children. My first was just a respecter of authority, so she's fine. But Bonnie is a total diva!' she sighs. 'Absolutely – just incredible tantrums. But I've learned after nine long years not to engage. And still when she has the occasional tantrum I just shut down and take myself away or whatever, and I don't get into it; I don't discuss it.'

However, Kaye admits it took her a while to learn this lesson and for a time she pandered to Bonnie's every need. 'She was so difficult,' she recalls. 'I mean, she would go crazy about the seam of her sock annoying one of her toes! And she would just kick off. I used to try and have a conversation and say stuff like "There's nothing wrong with your sock", "Do you want another pair of socks?", "What's wrong with it?", "Do you want a pair of tights?" "What do you want?!" but it would just get worse and worse. But now I know that the answer is – just step away from the child.'

Sound advice, Kaye, but Nadia has her own ways of trying to calm her kids down. Only, as she has discovered, her unorthodox methods don't always work out the way she'd like.

'I was on a plane coming back from somewhere ridiculous and I'd done the classic new, inexperienced mum thing of thinking I'd get a night flight because then Maddie would sleep all the way through it,' she recalls with a shudder. 'Anyway, everyone had bedded down, Mark was asleep and immediately snoring, but I could tell that a tantrum was brewing in Maddie, and I thought, "My God, what am I going to do?"'

Suddenly, Nadia hit upon an idea that has been passed down through the ages by nans everywhere, though perhaps not something that a doctor would recommend. 'I know, I'll put some whisky in her bottle, I thought! That's what grans have done for years,' she laughs. 'I was a desperate mother! So I put a drop of whisky in her bottle thinking that would get her to sleep. But guess what happened? Exactly what happens to me when I have whisky – she "danced" all night! I feel so bad about it now – what a ridiculous thing to do!'

LOOSE LESSONS

- Don't be scared to discipline your kids. Children need to learn when they have done something wrong and what is appropriate behaviour.

- Smacking is a no-no. Not only is it considered a form of abuse, it doesn't really work and only creates resentment and anger.

- If your child is having a full-on tantrum, don't try to pander to their demands as it really won't help you stop these fits of fury from happening in the future.

PARENTAL DILEMMAS

WHEN DO YOU BECOME TOO OVERLY PROTECTIVE?

We can't help it, but when our kids are out of sight we worry. What are they up to? Who are they with? What trouble could they be getting themselves into? It's an inescapable part of being a parent.

But of course, we too were once young and carefree, gallivanting out on the streets with our mates and causing our parents to worry their socks off. It's funny how priorities change, isn't it?

Although the world has always been a dangerous place, what with the amount of coverage in the press about terrorist attacks, stabbings and abductions, it feels like it's not safe to step foot out of the house. Is this making us into a nation of worriers and over protective parents who won't let their kids out of their sight? Should kids be allowed to have their freedom and be responsible for themselves?

'If we could get away with it, thinking our kids are going to love us forever, you'd wrap them up in bubble wrap and go, "You're not going out ever!"' Coleen says. 'However, the reality is, we have to give our children the room to breathe. We have brought them up to be good and sensible people, the least we can do is let them go out into the world and try to make it a better place.'

However, Jane understands why parents are scared to let their children out into a world where so many bad things happen. 'I read an article that said something like 88 per cent of children now see life through a car window, because we constantly ferry them from one place to another,' she explains. 'Once upon a time, when we were kids, our parents would say to us, "See you later, off you go and play." But we don't allow that any more, because of stories like Madeleine McCann's disappearance and others that make us risk averse.'

However, Jane says that in spite of all the horrific news we read in the press, she constantly tries to think with a sensible head and understand that while bad things do happen, you can't let fear stop you or your children from living a full and active life. Though her husband Gary is much more protective about their children. In fact, sometimes, their differences in opinion lead to arguments about what their daughters should be allowed to do.

'My husband is the polar opposite of me and sometimes that is the cause of arguments between us,' Jane reveals. 'My daughter was planning to go on a school trip to Paris a couple of years back. It was right after the *Charlie Hebdo* terrorist attacks by ISIS and my husband said to me, "Well she's obviously not going now." And I said, "Of course she's going, it's a school trip with her friends." He replied, "Well I don't want her to go." We ended up having this big argument and I told him there are terrorist attacks everywhere and we can't live our lives like that!'

In the end, the couple agreed that their daughter could join the trip after all. But even though Jane had put up a fight to reassure Gary that nothing would happen to their precious daughter, she admits she spent the entire time her daughter was away in constant fear of something terrible taking place. 'I was like, "Oh my God, please don't let anything happen," because I know that would have been a devastating loss and the end of our marriage, and not just that, he would have said, "I told you so!"'

Gloria recalls that living in Northern Ireland during the Troubles in the seventies and eighties she was always, understandably, extremely protective of her kids. 'There were bombs, bullets and barricades everywhere,' she reminisces. 'You never knew what was going to happen in pubs, and your priority was keeping the kids safe. So I would pick Caron up in the car because I didn't want her to take public transport. However, I discovered from a friend of hers after we lost Caron that she wasn't always doing what she had told me. She'd tell me she was at the Arts Theatre learning a script but really she was up the Falls Road in Belfast in a shebeen, which was an illegal pub, drinking away, having a ball.'

You'd think that now, with all the ways we are able to communicate with each other these days, we'd feel a lot more confident about our children's welfare. But Coleen says that even though having a mobile phone means she should be able to get hold of her kids whenever she wants to, she actually finds herself worrying about them even more.

'When we were kids, I'd go out of the house at seven in the morning. Mum would say "Remember dinner's on the table at six." And if you weren't home by then, your life wouldn't be worth living! But I don't think she ever worried about us until six o'clock. Whereas my kids go out at midday and I am texting them "Are you there yet?" and if they don't text me back instantly I'm mad with worry! And my boys are fully grown men!'

Jane thinks parents don't make it easy for kids to understand what we want from them because we give them so many mixed messages.

'We're our own worst enemies sometimes,' she says. 'We say to them, "I don't want you going there," and then "Will you get off that computer!", "Will you stop watching that television!", and they'll say to me, "I want to go out but you won't let me!"'

WHAT AGE CAN WE LEAVE OUR KIDS AT HOME ALONE?

Did you know that there isn't a legal age limit in place, up to which you're not allowed to leave kids alone? According to the The National Society for the Prevention of Cruelty to Children, the law doesn't actually state an age when you can officially leave a child on their own, but says it is an offence to leave a child alone if it places them at risk. Parents can be prosecuted if they leave a child unsupervised 'in a manner likely to cause unnecessary suffering or injury to health'. The NSPCC also states that children under 12 are rarely mature enough to be left alone for a long period of time and children under 16 shouldn't be left alone overnight. Babies, toddlers and very young children should NEVER be left alone.

And yet some parents do just that. Sometimes to quickly nip to the local shop, other times to go out for the night with their mates. There have even been cases when parents have jetted out of the country on a holiday leaving their under tens minding the fort.

Jane finds it astonishing that the rules have not been made clearer. 'The legislation around this is so woolly,' she says. 'The government say it's up to the parents to decide whether or not the child is safe at home, but certain local authorities have different ideas, as do the police, so it's very, very random. And if you think as a parent that your child is capable of staying home alone, you can apparently leave them at any age within reason, as long as they're not at risk.'

Of course, there are more risks facing home-alone kids than just accidental ones in the home like faulty wiring or gas leaks.

'You could leave a very sensible 11 year old at home and have somebody who is not very nice come to the door,' Jane continues. 'So in that case, you have therefore left your child at risk. See, it's all so very vague.'

Nadia thinks that no child should be left unattended, no matter how responsible you think he or she is.

'A sensible child might say one night, "I want a bagel" and then cut themselves while slicing it. That might be a perfectly sensible child, who might be fine with a bagel when you're there. But it really worries me because there is always that risk that something could go wrong and they could have a terrible accident and be left without help for hours or days. How would you be able to live with yourself if something went wrong?.'

However, while Nadia is concerned about the dangers within the home, she also reckons that when any parent lets their kids out of the house with their friends, there are even more risks to worry about.

'I think nine or ten year olds are far more at risk when they go out to the park,' she says. 'Some of my friends let their kids go to the park at ten, and I think, "Really?"'

Coleen, on the other hand, says parents have to be careful not to become paranoid and should give their children a little bit of space as they get older to grow and discover the world.

'When Ciara was 13 she started to crave a bit of independence and was spending a couple of hours in the local town with her group of mates,' she says. However, while Coleen was keen to let her youngest child start to enjoy the world around her, her husband of the time was much more cautious. 'Ray was the opposite of me and was worried about what could happen, but I felt it was important for her to be a bit more street wise, and to show her that we were giving her a bit more independence,' she says. 'That said, I wouldn't have left her at home on her own for hours – even though she was sensible. And I wouldn't leave a child as young as six on their own in the house either. Not even for ten minutes!'

SHOULD YOU LET YOUR KIDS HAVE A MESSY ROOM?

Is your child's messy bedroom the sign of a cluttered, disorganised mind or could it be an indicator that you have a creative star of the future in your midst? Most parents want their kids to be neat and tidy and so try to instil in them the need to clean up after themselves. But are we setting them up for orderly future lives or are we cramping their creative style?

Well, Nadia, a self-confessed clutterer reckons that every child should feel relaxed in their own personal space and says she sees people's bedrooms 'as a place for freedom of expression'. In fact, she whole heartedly encourages her daughters to live in a space they feel comfortable in.

'Maddie's room used to be messy and I would never say to her clear it up, not unless she's got people coming round,' she says. 'It's her space. It's her world. I just close the door.'

However, over the years Maddie and Kiki have bucked the house trend and become very tidy and organised. And Nadia feels somewhat perturbed. 'My daughters are a constant disappointment to me,' she giggles. 'They are tidy, they are sensible. I used to encourage them to be messy. I'd open the kitchen-cupboard doors and say take everything out and mix it. I used to look forward to coming downstairs and finding washing-up liquid everywhere. I ask Mark sometimes, where did we go wrong?'

Nadia reckons the girls' neatness is actually a rebellious reaction to her own messy nature. 'Every single night Kiki says, "I'm just going up to clear my room up, mum"' and I say, '"All right!" She's weird!' Nadia laughs. 'She does it every day – it's pin sharp, clean, it's immaculate. She lines her little shoes up, she dusts! I really can't get my head around it.'

Nadia probably finds her daughters' astonishing attention to detail rather alien because she is – as the other Loose Women attest – one of the messiest people you are ever likely to meet. However, this chaotic lifestyle she exists in also appears to be a rebellious reaction to her upbringing, during which she was forced by her super strict mum to tidy her room on a regular basis. Only, Nadia, being the creative-thinking rebel that she is, didn't exactly toe the line.

And did her mum's strict house rules teach her any lessons? In fact, it made her decidedly worse, she confesses. 'It taught me nothing, because I still am the messiest person. I like it when kids draw on the wall.'

Although the idea of drawing on walls appals Saira, Jane admits that she somewhat agrees with Nadia and says that because her youngest daughter Grace displayed an artistic flair, she agreed to let her get creative.

'Grace is very arty and Gary is very particular and very tidy. But in her room she can do what she wants,' Jane explains. 'She asked me if she could draw on the walls. I said why not, because if we sell the house we just have to paint over it. So she has graffiti; she's got clothes everywhere and we can just close the door on it. Everyone needs their sanctuary.'

Saira admits hearing Nadia and Jane's rather progressive attitude to tidiness makes her feel queasy. 'I am very particular. I think I have been like that since an early age. We have just had the house renovated and I have given the kids some rules like, "When you walk up the stairs, hold the bannister. Why do you need to touch the walls?" Even their bedrooms are tidy. I say to them, "I am paying the mortgage, it's my room, not yours. One day you can do it to your own space." People like Nadia and Jane are saying just live in a tip. I just couldn't shut the door on it. I would be lying in bed worrying about it. Children are animals who need to be trained.'

However, as unorthodox as she can be, Jane does draw the line when it comes to leaving food lying around their rooms. 'My daughter is terrible for it – my God,' Jane sighs. 'Botulism in our house. She once left a bagel on top of the radiator in her room. I found it covered in mould. She told me it was a science experiment.'

However, Kaye blames herself in part for her daughters' behaviour as she says some of the meals she prepares for them don't go down too well because, basically, she's rubbish in the kitchen.

'She would hide food like fish that she didn't like and to be fair I can't blame her, because I can't cook,' she says. 'There was this one time, I made a bit of boiled white fish and she said, "I'm not having that." So, unbeknown to me, she stuffed it down between the couch and the radiator. Four weeks later, something started to smell a little bit and I thought I was going to have to get pest control in. And then I found it – this decomposing haddock!'

Jane recalls how her daughter's habit of leaving food on the floor attracted unwanted pests. 'When my middle daughter was 17 or something, we found a dead mouse under her cupboard and that was the turning point for us,' she says. Jane made it crystal clear to her girls that leaving food and mess around the house would only encourage more whiskered friends to move in with them and her daughters soon learned their lesson and were more careful about what they left lying around.

Now Jane thinks she's hit upon a great idea for parents of messy children to encourage their kids to be more responsible about their surroundings: 'If you have an untidy child, just get a dead mouse from anywhere and plant it!'

SHOULD WE KEEP A CHECK ON OUR KIDS' PHONES?

Everyone deserves privacy. But as our kids grow up, should we be keeping more of an eye on them and scrutinising what they are getting up to, especially on social media where they can be exposed to the dubious characters who are lurking in cyberspace?

Nadia says she wishes she had been more vigilant with her oldest daughter's mobile-phone use when she was younger. She subsequently made sure that she was all over her younger daughter's online activity to ensure that nobody with any dodgy intentions was able to interact with her child.

'I have to admit, I used to feel awkward asking to check Maddie's phone because I'd left it too late with her. It felt wrong to ask her for her password. It's not that I didn't trust her, I do. I trust her implicitly; it's the sharks swimming out there around them I don't trust. They're the ones whom I worry about,' she explains. 'But I did it differently with my younger daughter Kiki and I have her password so she knows I can have a look. I won't be a maniac checking it, and I won't be checking on her. I'm checking on what other people are showing and saying.'

Jane says she is also very hands-on with her kids' social-media activity and has always demanded her daughters' passwords so she can make sure that there's nothing to worry about. 'I had my youngest's Instagram feed on my phone and I used to check it regularly, I think you have to when they are young,' Jane says. 'You have to step away when you know they're mentally able to deal with stuff they may see online, though.'

However, she does admit that sometimes having access to her daughters' Instagram feed has led to some embarrassing moments for them. 'One Mother's Day, we went out to the local pub for a Sunday roast, and the Yorkshire pudding was so huge, it was like a planet; so I just had to Instagram it when we got home,' she remembers. 'Then my youngest daughter burst into the kitchen saying, "Oh my God, mum, what have you done?!" I'd forgotten that I'd been on her Instagram. So I'd posted it on her account! She said she'd had hundred of messages from her friends calling her a loser and saying #SundayRoast was so lame! She didn't speak to me for the rest of the afternoon.'

Nadia says she regrets giving in to her daughters' relentless requests to own mobile phones early on and reckons that mums need to stick together and not give in to pressure from their kids. Aside from the fear that children can be chatting to dubious characters online, she is also scared that they will begin to use their imaginations less.

'Daydreaming is so important as a kid. I don't see my kids daydreaming like we used to do,' she says. 'They go straight back to the phone to see how many "likes" they have. That's so sad.'

However, as it's too late for her to change her daughters' phone habits she says all she can do now is to make them aware of the many dangers that they can come across online and encourage them to be as honest with her as possible. 'It comes down to having an open conversation with your kids,' Nadia says. 'They're not going to tell you everything. But if you keep telling them about the danger of porn or violent sites then you're giving them all the right information so that they can keep safe and alert.'

Meanwhile, Gloria says she would dearly love the younger generation to tear themselves away from their tablets and explore the world just like she used to do as a kid. 'I love to see kids out building cubbies and putting up tents, as opposed to sitting inside on a bloody computer. I remember, for hours, we would go out on our bikes into the country. My dad never drove and so we were always on bicycles. I sometimes just feel quite sad that some children never get the chance to do what I would call ordinary, natural, healthy things. But then I grew up in very different and somehow more innocent days in Northern Ireland.'

SHOULD WE POST PHOTOS OF OUR KIDS WITHOUT THEIR PERMISSION?

Not so long ago, many of us would painstakingly stick our most cherished photographs into a photo album, before packing it away and forgetting all about it. Photo albums have now become a rarity as we tend to take pictures on our camera phones and rarely print them. Therefore, a lot of us tend to use social-media platforms to document our lives. Many of us are happy to post personal images from family holidays and their kids' birthday celebrations on Facebook or Instagram for all the world to see. But is it right that we post personal pics of our children online without their consent? Or should they be kept private away from dubious eyes...?

Janet Street-Porter is adamant that pictures of people's children should never be posted online until the kids are of an age when they can give approval, and are old enough to understand the implications. She also reckons that by sharing personal images of them, children's parents are ultimately 'stealing their childhood'.

'I feel really, really strongly about posting pictures of children under the age of consent and before they are legally able to control their lives,' she says. 'The way I see it, parents have stolen their childhood – and these kids could look back when they are 16, 17, 18 and might have a different view about what you're doing now. The pictures of my childhood are in an album, but now people feel it's perfectly OK to share pictures with people they'll never meet.'

Saira, on the other hand, has a different take on posting personal pictures publicly, as she considers it an extension of her TV persona.

'I use social media for inspiration, for motivation, and my followers want to see what I'm like, not just on telly, but behind the scenes,' she says. 'I'm a mother, so I do post pictures of the family like, "This is us on holiday", "This is what I'm giving the kids for breakfast", "This is how I get rid of their dry skin"; "This is Zac growing up".'

However, even though she includes many pictures of her children online she says as she's their mum she doesn't need to seek their approval. 'I don't ask them about posting their pictures,' she explains. 'But I don't ask them what they want for breakfast either. They are both young and I'm their parent. So far they've never ever said, "Oh mum, that's really embarrassing, don't post that!"'

Jane says she understands Saira's interest in sharing images with her followers but is hesitant about the broad availability of them on public forums like Instagram. 'You see, the way I see it is that Saira's children aren't making that decision about posting those pictures,' she muses. 'I wouldn't object so much if she were doing it on Facebook or through a closed circuit, but you're actually putting them out there to people you don't know, whom you're never going to meet. I just find it a bit creepy!'

Saira, however, doesn't share Jane or Janet's cynical stance and says she's more open minded about society than them. 'I don't see the world as a negative, bad place – my followers follow me – it's about sharing who you are, and if you don't want to do it, don't be on social media,' she says.

However, having taken their views on board she admits that perhaps she should start thinking about the bigger picture and be more cautious about posting her family's life online. 'I think perhaps sometimes I see the world as an innocent, naive place and that all my followers are lovely, but I think I do have to take some responsibility. I will take that on board.'

ARE YOU READY FOR THE KIDS TO LEAVE HOME?

For years you've joked about the day your kids finally get out from under your feet and move out of your house. But when that time comes, the gravity of their departure can hit you like a slap in the face as you come to realise that the house will no longer be filled with the sound of your kids calling out, "Mum, where are my jeans?" or "Mum, what time is dinner?" While those questions asked on repeat for years might have bugged the life out of you, now that the kids have gone, you can't help but suddenly feel those good old-fashioned 'empty-nest blues'.

Coleen says that when her two sons were working away for a year she suddenly realised how much she missed them. 'I'd gone through that stage of thinking, "God, if I find one more wet towel on the bed, or boxers on the floor, or cups with mould in..."' she reminisces. 'And when they left I was like, "I can clean their rooms – and they're going to stay clean!" Then after a few days of them being away I thought, "I want to see wet towels." I'd even go in and put boxers on the floor! It was a lonely time of my house being clean, and I wanted them to come home and mess it up.'

Gloria agrees that when Caron and her son Paul left home at the same time to go to uni and drama college, she was devastated. 'It was like a bereavement,' she recalls. 'Up until then, my day had been planned around them leaving for school, picking them up, what am I going to cook, things like that. And both of them were away and I was at a loss. Also, I had got so used to their friends coming around all the time that I would miss them too. I missed the noise and all the fun around the house.'

Kaye says as she watches her girls get older and more independent she has begun to feel lonelier, even though they are actually still in the house with her. 'Everyone must relate to that moment when you bring them home in that little seat and for the first two years you never go to the toilet alone! But funnily enough, as they get older, they want to be their own person and have their own mates and I'm the most embarrassing person in the world, so I'm a bit lonely inside now because I miss the relationship we used to have.'

Kaye says she understands that it is a natural rite of passage for kids to fly the nest but admits she will be heartbroken when they go. 'It's the way it's meant to be. I remember my mum was upset but she didn't overdo it. Charly will leave school next year and she will go to uni and move out and I am dreading that. When I was ready to leave home I was off. And I imagine my daughter will be too.'

LOOSE LESSONS

- Of course we worry about our kids surviving in the real world, but remember what we were like when we were their age! Just always make sure that they know they can talk to you about anything.

- If your child has a messy room, you can either assert your authority and get them to tidy up pronto or see their clutter as artistic expression and rebellion!

- It will be tough when your kids come to leave home, but it is all part of the natural process of growing up and you should embrace and enjoy this next stage.

PART 3
GO LOVE YOURSELF

Now here's a question...who in the world do you love most? Is it your other half? Your kids? Your parents? Almost impossible to pick, right? But what about you? Do you actually love yourself? Do you love the person you are?

It might sound like a weird question. After all, a lot of us rarely ever think of ourselves unless it is to criticise something we don't like. You know, like, 'I could do with losing a couple of inches from my waist', 'My hair needs a rethink', 'Should I really be going for that promotion?' We are so overly critical about ourselves that we often forget to appreciate the really great aspects about us that others notice and value. But as hard as it might sound (and perhaps it feels a bit uncomfortable too), it is important that we do start to learn to love ourselves. If you are spending too much time looking at the worst aspects of yourself, how you will ever find the time to see the best things in other people?

Nobody is perfect. It's a fact! Even the most gorgeous celebrities can find things about themselves that they wish they could change. So instead of pouring scorn on all the bits of ourselves we don't like, why don't we go ahead and celebrate the positive aspects. Think about all the things you love about yourself, no matter how big or small. You'll be surprised just how many positive things there are.

THE WAY WE LOOK

HAVE YOU BEEN JUDGED ON YOUR LOOKS?

We can't help it, but we all do it, right? We know we shouldn't but sometimes we can't not base our first impressions of someone on the way they dress, speak or style their hair. For example, take a handsome fella with immaculate stubble wearing a sharp suit; what instantly springs to mind? That he's successful? Rich? Well travelled? Or is he just a clever chancer blagging his way through life?

While it is sometimes true that the way people look can indeed match a certain personality trait, not everyone can be judged on face value. It might sound like a tired cliché, but it is true: you really can't judge a book by its cover. And when it happens to us, well, we get annoyed, especially if the way we are perceived by others is not the way we actually are or want to be seen.

It may come as a surprise, but even our open-minded Loose Ladies can judge people from time to time by the way they sound and look, as Janet reveals...

'I definitely formed an opinion of Stacey when I first met her,' she says of the time she came face to face with the former *X Factor* singer Stacey Solomon. 'She was nervous and hyperventilating, and I thought, "She's so smart and she's got such a good voice, but what's she really like?" It's interesting because you do make snap judgements. And coming from west London, I had an opinion about her accent.'

Janet is certainly no stranger to people judging her based on her accent – for years, impressionists took great pleasure in mimicking her very distinctive voice. 'I really experienced it when I started out on the radio. People were outraged that I could have a daily radio show in

London with a London accent. They were absolutely disgusted.'

Janet says she thinks these days people are judged more on the way they sound than the way they look. 'You seem to be judged in modern Britain the minute you open your mouth and people think you're stupid or thick if you've got a working-class or London accent,' she says. 'Years ago, I did a late-night TV show with Clive James and Russell Harty, and one day I was talking to Russell about opera when Clive just turned to me and said, "I didn't think people like you went to the opera." And I'd been going to the opera with my godmother from the age of about nine or ten. I was totally offended! I nearly said, "I probably know more about the opera than you do!" I felt so strongly about judging people by their accents.'

Janet believes even now there are still too few London accents like hers on the airwaves. 'On the BBC, in particular, all you hear is Welsh accents, Scottish accents and Irish accents. You don't hear accents like mine on Radio 4 or BBC One.'

And legendary presenter and radio host Gloria Hunniford knows all too well about the celebration of certain dialects as she admits to landing her radio gig on Radio 2 at a time when regional accents reigned.

'When Terry Wogan was on Radio 2, the Irish accent became very popular,' she remembers. 'And in fact I was in on the back of that and Ken Bruce had a Scottish accent. And Terry always said that the Irish accent meant – particularly in England – that you were classless because nobody knew where you were from. I was very lucky in reverse.'

Gloria also says that she was lucky in the early days that she got to meet a radio producer who didn't judge her by the way she looked and took a risk on her becoming a serious broadcaster.

Back then she was trying to forge a career as a singer. After appearing as a guest on the Northern Irish equivalent of Radio 4's *Today* programme, the show's producer called her up to ask her if she had ever considered being a news reporter, which she hadn't. Excited by the offer she landed the job, at a time when there were very few female employees in Northern Irish radio.

'On the first day I was there, the producer showed me around and asked me, "What do you see in the newsroom?" And I said I see a lot of men pounding away on typewriters. And he said, "Remember, as a woman you're not coming in here to do the knitting and the sewing and the recipes. You'll be as good as any bloke sitting in this room, and you'll be out on the streets of Northern Ireland reporting on bombs, bullets and barricades like the rest." So from my point of view, I've never had to worry about sexism. What a forward-looking man.'

However, she says she can be judgemental herself when it comes to the way some people present themselves. 'Glamour seems to be secondary these days,' she explains. 'When I first started to go to the theatre in London visiting from Northern Ireland, I would have worn a long dress, it was such an event. But now you see people in cut-off shirts and lots of tattoos, and that's just horrible. So at times I suppose I do tend to judge people a bit.'

Meanwhile, Saira admits that she has a terrible habit of judging people. 'I admit it, I do judge people by the way they look and carry themselves,' she confesses. 'I was brought up with the mentality that you have to be the best you can. I myself have been judged on the colour of my skin, my gender, so you'd think I'd be less judgemental. But it's human nature. There have been so many times when I have told myself not to judge a book by its cover. I am not perfect. But I have always instilled in my kids that they should not judge people.'

SHOULD WE DRESS 'AGE APPROPRIATELY'?

When we get older should we really start dressing our age? Over the past year or so, the likes of 50-plus women like Helena Christensen have been criticised for wearing clothes that were deemed too young. (Helena stylishly wore a sexy bustier to an event.) So should we think twice about wearing something that you might see on a star of *Love Island*?

The best advice is to always wear what you feel comfortable in, something that makes your body look its best. Some women of a certain age can pull off very young trends – look at 51-year-old Kylie Minogue, who is still dressing like a woman half her age but looks truly amazing.

Our Loose Women admit they have become increasingly cautious when it comes to fashion as the years drift by, but believe that we let what other people say cloud our judgement.

'I think we place the restrictions on ourselves,' Jane says. 'I don't think anyone would ever say to us, "You can't wear that." But there are certain things I just won't wear. I won't wear miniskirts any more. I just think it's not age appropriate. Those over-the-knee boots. My daughter's got a pair of them and she looks fantastic in them. I tried a pair on, and I looked like a menopausal fisherman! It just looked ridiculous so I put them straight back again.'

However, she says that her daughter is always encouraging her to dress a little younger. 'She's pushes me to dress a bit more trendy or whatever. Mostly because I'm always in jeans and a dog-walking coat! So no, the restrictions are what I place on myself.'

However, Janet thinks age restriction is a load of baloney and that women should absolutely wear what they want! 'I think this notion of age-appropriate clothes is something that has been dreamed up recently,' she says. 'Women should wear what the hell they like. Madonna looks great! Remember that a lot of these fashion designers use 14-year-old girls to promote their products. You have schoolchildren holding a handbag worth three thousand quid.'

Janet, who is stylish in her seventies, is renowned for clothes that are cool and edgy, so it comes as no surprise to hear she would never worry about feeling too old to wear something as long as she felt comfortable in it. 'Do I judge myself? No, my main thing is how big does my backside look or will I have to hold my stomach in all day.'

SHOULD WE AVOID MIRRORS?

Mirrors are funny things, aren't they? You think they're telling you the truth, but you're seeing a slightly skewed image of yourself that sometimes you like and other times – particularly in department-store changing rooms – you might absolutely hate.

The biggest problem is when we stand in front of a mirror we're never looking out for our best aspects. Instead, we are trying to seek out the bits we don't like so we can do something about them before anyone else lays eyes on us. But the more we do that, the more things we see that we don't like. By the time we've finished looking at ourselves, we're probably feeling so insecure, ugly and antisocial that we just want to throw off our clothes, and jump into bed and hide under the duvet until our fairy godmother sprinkles some magic dust over us to make us look Hollywood pretty.

If this sounds like you, then don't worry – you're not the only one who has a problem with reflective surfaces. So too does Nadia, who says she hates mirrors so much so that she has hardly any in her house.

'None of us has any mirrors in the bedroom, and we don't really have a big one,' she explains. 'My daughter keeps asking me for a full-length one and I keep thinking about whether to get one or not.'

So what has made Nadia hate mirrors so much? Well, as she explains, it goes back to the days when she wasn't happy with her body. 'Because I've had so many issues with my weight over the years, whenever I passed a mirror, I would just criticise myself,' she says. 'When we're in a hotel and we're all dressed up, I think I look pretty hot – I get into a lift and I'm surrounded by mirrors and I feel deflated.'

Kaye thinks Nadia should face her fears and undergo what she describes as 'mirror therapy'. 'We should all stand in front of a full-length mirror every morning and just learn to accept ourselves,' she explains. 'Appearance is important, and we should enjoy how we look and be happy with who we are. We have to learn to love ourselves.'

LOOSE LESSONS

- Dress how you feel most comfortable. You may become more conservative as you get older or you may just want to ignore the doubters – do whatever makes you feel your best.

- Always love yourself. Don't focus on the bits you don't like, instead find the parts of you that you want to celebrate and make you feel good.

- You won't feel good all the time and you will have moments of insecurity, which is fine. Tomorrow is a fresh new day!

THE WAY WE FEEL

FEELING INVISIBLE AS YOU GET OLDER

  Let's face it, we live in a world that worships youth. Advertisers and TV companies busy themselves chasing the youth market while older people tend to be ignored. So as we get older and pass the age that we feel society considers no longer sexy, do we imagine we are fading into the background and becoming invisible?

Coleen most definitely thinks that when she turned a half-century she became a mere shadow of her former self, especially now that she's back dating again.

'I do feel a bit invisible after 50, especially now I'm single,' she says. 'I do think, "Who is going to interested in me when they can get a 30 or 40 year old?" I sometimes wonder where I fit in now because who will I be attractive to? The thing is, you don't plan to get into your fifties, or almost mid-fifties and be single – I think that's what made me feel a bit invisible to the world.'

However, Coleen says that at this stage in life, she's actually not so fussed about finding new love in a hurry. Not yet, anyway! 'It's amazing when you become single, people instantly want you to meet someone, but in actual fact, I'm really happy to have this time of just being me, because I haven't had that for years,' she reasons. 'My house is always full of the kids and their friends and the animals, so I don't feel lonely. But when they all go out I do have five minutes when I miss them and worry about not having that companionship.'

That said, every time the realisation hits her that she's the mum of children in their late twenties and thirties, she's reminded that she is indeed no longer a spritely spring chicken.

'Shane Jr's in his early thirties, and I thought to myself recently, "I'm way too young to have a 30 year old, I don't think he's mine",' she laughs. 'But if I'm honest, I loved every previous decade of my life. I never understood people saying, "I hate getting older, I don't want to celebrate it, don't buy me cards." But that was until I got to my fifties. And I've hated it since then.'

Janet, on the other hand, doesn't agree with Coleen in the slightest. And why would she? 'I don't feel invisible in the slightest,' she declares. 'You're not invisible in your fifties; life's what you make it. And I'd say to anyone watching who's starting to feel invisible: get up in the morning and make the day what you want it to be. Just be confident.'

Coleen agrees with Janet's enthusiastic take on life but admits that as her kids are getting older and don't appear to need her as much, she can't help feeling a little bit at a loss. 'Ciara's now 17, she's just passed her driving test so she's off. And you sit at home and think, "Oh, my job is done" because they don't really need me,' she sighs. 'I mean, your kids always need you, but they're very independent now.'

Jane reckons Coleen has reached a time in her life when she should start thinking about giving her life a bit of a rebrand.

'The time is right for you to reboot your life,' she advises. 'You need to start telling yourself, "OK, so I'm not needed so much there, so what am I going to do for me?" I think we all go through that.'

Gloria says that she and her Loose Women are lucky to be doing what they do. 'We are lucky we are in the business we are in,' she says. 'It seems to attract a lot of attention, so I don't feel socially invisible. We are all strong women and we can hold our own. Also I have been on daily programmes for many years and in the main people tend to regard me as part of their family, so there is an automatic friendship.'

Jane admits that while she never feels invisible at home, she has on occasions felt like she was unnoticed. 'I do feel that Gary listens to me and my kids listen to me. So that's great. But there have been situations socially where I don't feel as listened to as I might have been when I was younger. I do feel more invisible socially. However, go to Spain, where older people are treated with great reverence.'

WHAT'S THE KEY TO CONFIDENCE?

Just because someone strides across the room like they own it, it doesn't necessarily mean they feel like they do. People can actually be riddled with unseen insecurities. Confidence is something that is very elusive for many of us.

'I know people will think we're all super confident because we sit here and we spout away, but even someone like me has a whole lot of insecurities going on inside,' Janet confesses. 'I might seem confident if you came up to me on the Underground or in the street. But I do have nightmares where I feel I'm not going to look good enough to attend a party I've been invited to and I'll just slink into the background.'

As hard as it is to believe that the celebrated TV producer and journalist ever lacks confidence, she explains that she thinks her tough upbringing in west London is partly responsible for her insecurities. 'I am from a working-class background and coming from this background and going on to be successful makes me feel deep down that I'm being judged because I haven't come from the right background.'

She adds: 'I've been mocked over my accent, my teeth, my hair, looking funny. Don't feel sorry for me, I don't want your pity! I can quite happily deliver a speech on stage as long as I have my bullet points. But ask me to the pub at six and I will demand that the person I'm meeting is there before me because I would just die if I opened the door and walked into a room of people I didn't know.'

Coleen says that we all have the power to make others believe we haven't got a care in the world. 'You have to blag confidence sometimes,' she says. 'You have to say to yourself, "I'm feeling so insecure and scared about this, but I'm just going to do it."'

Nadia admits that she used to find it hard to blag confidence because she wasn't happy about her weight. However, she says that she used her anger at her weight as a way to deal with things going wrong. 'When I was young, I was paranoid about the way I looked,' she explains. 'I was heavier and I think I held on to my weight to protect myself from failure. I'd go on diets and when I'd get to the last ten pounds I'd start eating again. That way I had something to blame when things didn't work out and I could tell myself, "Well, that didn't happen because I was overweight!"'

But her skewed view of her body and her confidence led to her missing out on the role of a lifetime on a huge Hollywood blockbuster! 'Years ago, when I was acting, I had just shot a movie and the producer of it called me afterwards and asked me to fly out to Rome to meet Ridley Scott about a role in the movie *Gladiator*,' she recalls. 'I was very excited of course, and should have said to myself what every other actress would have told themselves: "I'm going out there, I've practically got the part. This is a dream come true." But I didn't. Instead, the first thing I said to myself was, "I can't do this because I'm too fat." And do you know what I did? I told the producer I was shooting a big series, which meant I couldn't go. So I missed out on starring in a massive blockbuster because I let my lack of confidence get the better of me. Now there's a lesson of what not to do.'

NADIA'S LETTER TO HER TEENAGE SELF

What with dealing with busy jobs, looking after a family and trying to make time to catch up with friends, we rarely have time to sit back and reflect on our lives. After all, by the time we've made it our thirties, forties and fifties, so much has passed that we don't get to appreciate all the things that we have achieved and discovered about ourselves or reflect on what's changed around us. In fact, life goes so quickly that we really do have to take a pause to look at what has happened. And what better way is there to do that than to write a letter to your teenage self? It might sound like a strange thing to do, but it is a really lovely idea that gets you to reflect on the life that has flown by and reminds you what a wonderful person you have become. It can also be an emotional experience, especially if your life has changed considerably for the better. Look back on your life and identify those key things you've done that you thought at 16 would be impossible? Look back at how you dealt with the tough times you thought might break you; the events that changed your life for the better and for the worse. Remember the people you met who set you on various paths, the decisions you made that were wise and those that weren't quite so sensible, but that you have since learned lessons from.

Still not quite sure what to write? Well, perhaps Nadia's retrospective letter might be of some help.

Dear Nadia

You will waste a lifetime worrying about what everyone else thinks of you. You will drink and party far too much to try and shut up those nasty little voices in your head. But trust me, you will rather joyfully get to a place where you worry more about what you think of everyone else rather than what they think of you. Unfortunately this won't happen until your fifties. You will also discover that whatever money you spend on trying to rid yourself of cellulite will be money down the drain.

See? Here Nadia has acknowledged the ups-and-downs in her roller-coaster life, and in doing so she acknowledges how she has been able to embrace them and carry on to become the strong and independent-thinking woman we all know and love.

A letter to your teenage self is a perfect way of seeing how far you have come and, if you're in a life rut, to understand that you can once again work your way out of any problems.

DOES NOT DRINKING MAKE YOU BORING?

Remember in *Friends* when Monica was going out with Fun Bobby, the tall, handsome guy who was only a hoot when he had a drink in him and deadly dull when he hadn't? A lot of us love a drink on a night out but what with the health risks that we are warned constantly about and the irritating weight gains a few glasses of wine can cause is it wiser for us to swap the grog for a glass of water or a tasty cup of tea?

If it feels like drinking is an integral part of our social lives it can seem daunting to just quit. After all, there is nothing worse than being sober as a judge and having to watch your mates talk a lot of drunken, slurring nonsense. But could that make us seem... boring?

Coleen points out that drinking is such a key part of British culture that if anyone says they prefer not to they are often eyed with suspicion. 'As soon as you go anywhere and they go, "What do you want to drink?" and you say, "Actually I don't drink, I'll just have a cup of tea or a glass of orange," they look at you like you're some kind of alien,' she says. 'And what I want to say to them is: you class me as dull because I'm not drinking, which in your mind obviously means I can't party. But I'm always the last one standing and dancing and having a great time, but I feel good and I know where I am. But they never think that they're dull. And yet the drunker they get, they get so dull, so boring and so ridiculous.'

Nadia agrees that she's come across a lot of folk who think it's odd, even antisocial when someone says they don't drink. 'You are treated like a bit of a leper if you don't drink,' she says. 'Mark and I get invited to parties and because they know Mark is a recovering alcoholic and has been sober for years, they will say, "Mark won't want to come, will he, because he's not drinking?" And I think to myself, why? He still loves to talk to people and to dance and have a good time.'

DOES GETTING OLDER MAKE YOU SELFISH?

We've talked about how society's perception of older women can sometimes make us feel invisible, and we have also looked at how we can stop and take stock of the things we have achieved and endured that have shaped us into the people we are today. Because it's certainly true what they say – with age comes wisdom. Plus a certain pragmatism.

Loose Woman Ruth Langsford recently said that hubby Eamonn Holmes made the point that they have less time left ahead of them than they have behind them; that they should spend as much of that time packing good things into their remaining lives. Actor Michael Douglas has said that the upside of ageing is that 'you choose how to spend your time much more carefully... because you know it's finite'. Is this sound advice? Is it a good idea to focus on you and your pleasure when we start to get toward retirement age? Or is it selfish of us, particularly if we have families who still need our help?

Janet says she has never heard of such a ridiculous thing – she is living her life as it comes and not making plans for the time she has left.

'That's such a negative load of misery,' she says firmly. 'I'm 73 years old and I do not wake up in the morning and think, "Right, I am going to live to be 100, which means I've got 28 more summer holidays to plan, and after that I'm going to cark it."'

Instead, she says, she kicks off her day hoping it will be a good one, and checking things off a 'to do' list. 'I don't have a bucket list of things I'm going to do before I drop off or onto the other side,' she laughs. 'It's important to get up every day and think, "This is going to be a fantastic day and I'm going to do the best I can with it."'

While Janet might be renowned for her wonderfully grumpy demeanour she does admit that as she gets older she's trying new things in life – like being friendly and sociable with people. 'I am trying to be as smiley as I can be – I'm making progress on that,' she says. 'I talk to new people every day, although I do tend to shout at cyclists who get too close to where I'm walking on the way to work.'

However, Coleen adds that as she has got older, she has found the confidence to say no to things. Whereas in our youth we'd feel obliged to say yes to people around us, when you get older, you find yourself realising that you can say no because your own life has much more going on in it. 'I think it definitely comes with age,' she says. 'I don't think it's necessarily selfish, but you prioritise more without fear of repercussions. I'm always a people pleaser, but as time's gone on... well, I like to think about me!'

Gloria says that as she gets older she is embracing life as fully as she did when she was younger, if not more so. 'I am the oldest on the panel at the wrong end of 70, but my zest for work is still as keen as ever – I am signed up for shows that have been commissioned until 2022! I just want to do it all: I want to learn something new every day, meet new people; I want to do everything.'

DOES BEING NICE WORK?

The cynical among us say nice guys come last, that conniving, manipulative and devious so-and-sos always succeed. But is that true? Who knows for sure. No doubt we can all think of examples of those who shout the loudest and are in it for themselves, who have gone on to be successful, and the modest ones who don't rock the boat and who haven't risen up the ranks as fast, although they are just as good at their jobs.

Certainly it's not always possible to be nice, to let others have opportunities first. We're asking for trouble! To some, being nice is a green light for others to take advantage. In the workplace, for example, you can be a 'nice' boss, but there will still be times when you have to be firm, not take any nonsense, so that things get done and no one goes rogue. And the same can be said for friendships too. Of course we all try to be kind, but equally there will always be people who have a tendency to take the mick and exploit that nice nature of yours.

Janet, who is known for her 'takes-no-prisoners' attitude, says it is important to be nice but also to be assertive and not be a walkover. 'I am actually nice,' she says. 'I come with a frosty exterior, I've got quite an austere demeanour... but I do object when things aren't done right. That said, I don't raise my voice, I do it in a kind but firm way. Like recently, I was in a restaurant and I asked for a glass of wine and it didn't come and I couldn't find the waitress so I just got up, wandered round the restaurant and was virtually in the kitchen asking, "Where's my wine?"'

Coleen says being nice is a wonderful quality and makes her feel happier. 'I absolutely think it's always nice to be nice,' she says. 'I would rather people walk away and go, "Oh, she was nice," rather than, "Oh, she was an old bag!" And I do think people are more willing if you're nice to them, especially in shops or if they're serving you. You get a better service if you're a nice customer. I agree if it's bad service, you have every right to complain. But even when you're complaining, there's a nice way to do it. You don't have to scream and shout.'

There is one form of this that Janet says she simply can't abide, though: the scripted 'fake niceness' you get in the service industry. So if you work in a supermarket or coffee shop and you see Janet come in, just say 'hi' and 'bye' and forget about all the fluffy bits. She won't appreciate it!

'We have this fake niceness, when you walk into a shop and the cashier says something like, "How's your day been so far?" I say, "I won't go into it, I'm not going to tell you about my blood pressure, just as I don't want to know about your corns"'

Overly intrusive shop assistants are not Janet's only bugbear. 'The other thing that really annoys me, especially on the Underground, is when you see families with teenage children, where the carriage is absolutely packed, and women have got shopping bags or older people or pregnant women are standing up, and these kids of 13, 14 years old are occupying a seat. I said to some parents the other day, "Would you mind letting your children stand up?" She said, "They bought a ticket." No!'

LOOSE LESSONS

- It's easy to feel invisible as you get older, but it doesn't have to be that way! Enjoy the confidence and knowledge that comes with age.

- It is OK to sometimes feel insecure. Everyone occasionally feels out of their depth. Just fake it until you feel it.

- Being nice isn't boring and always being pleasant to people can get you things that being rude never will.

PART 4
FRIENDS AND FRENEMIES

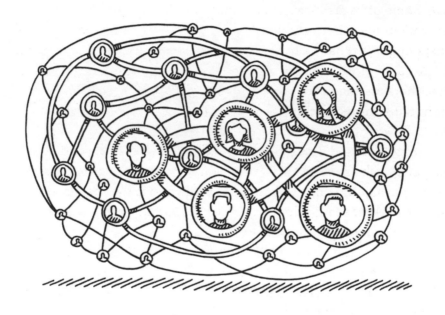

What would we do without our mates? For one, we'd have no one to gossip with. There'd be no one to help us pick up the pieces of our various love/career/family disasters, no one to go shopping with, to go on a night out with, no one to listen to our innermost secrets. There'd be no one to turn to at our lowest moments, no one to laugh with when we're riding high. So friends are a brilliant, essential part of life.

Of course, there are no rules as to how many friends you should have. Some of us are lucky enough to have picked up pals from all parts of our lives, from childhood through to the present day, while others might just have a handful of people that they keep close. Some will be super close, the type of friend you will open your heart to. Then there are the friends who are always great on a night out, but might not know you so well as your real besties. Or the friends you chat to at work but might not see outside of the office.

Or that loyal and devoted friend who knows you inside and out. The person who is there for you 24/7, knows absolutely everything about what's going on in that mind of yours and is the keeper of your deepest, darkest secrets. In many cases, your relationship with your best friend is stronger than the bond you have with your partner because they're the one you can confide in about absolutely anything – including moans about your other half – and have it go no further.

Occasionally, though, friendships can be a rocky ride – sometimes your best friend might not like your current boyfriend; other times, he or she may offer an opinion or judgement that you won't want to hear. And in some extreme cases, someone whom you thought was your friend might let you down in a way you never thought they would. Many of us have experienced a situation like this, and it can really hurt.

Take a look around you and write down a list of your friends. Break them into groups – best friends, social friends, work mates and so on. And the next time you feel lonely – we all do, so don't be ashamed – whip out that list and reassure yourself that you have an extended family of guys and girls who will always have your back.

GOOD FRIENDS

IS THERE ANYTHING WRONG WITH HAVING A SMALL GROUP OF FRIENDS?

As we talked about earlier, there is no rule about how many friends you're supposed to have. Having two good friends you trust with your life is far better than twenty superficial pals who barely know you and are only around for the fun times.

Friendship is what you make of it. If you want a big circle of people who are always up for a night out, then go ahead. But if you are seeking confidantes and people who will selflessly look out for you then that's your perogative too.

Janet admits she has been lucky to have accumulated lots of friends over the years from all her many activities. However, she says that as fond as she is of them, she has to be careful about mixing them. Like family members, they don't always gel, so it's important to make sure there are no irritating and unnecessary bust-ups!

'I've got loads and loads of friends and they go back through all the decades of my life. I mean, I'm not friends with anyone I went to school with, but I've got friends I was at college with, who I still go on holiday with. And then I've got friends from all the jobs I've ever done in the media and so on. But I did learn a lesson early on that you want your friends to be like your family but they're all not going to get on with each other. So it's best to keep them in groups.'

Gloria says that she has various groups of pals, all of whom offer different forms of friendship. 'I have friends whom I can call on immediately if I'm in trouble, friends I would have dinner with and friends I tend to meet casually at events,' she says. 'But I think as you get older you become more discerning about your friends. When

Caron died, some of my pals – well two in particular – just didn't give me what I needed (which sounds a bit selfish, but I was in such a black space). However, there were other friends who just gave me more than I could hope for and still do.'

Meanwhile, Coleen says that she can tell in a short space of time whether she will get on with a new person, probably because she grew up with five sisters. 'I can tell within the first hour or two of meeting someone whether they could be my friend,' she says. 'I've met people and after 20 minutes we've just clicked. I consider all the Loose Women my friends, but we've all got other really close, lifelong friends we could phone in the middle of the night if we needed them. And you also have friends who you have for a few years, and then you just don't gel any more. And that's hard.'

But even though she has a sizeable circle of pals, Coleen says there are just a handful of friends she considers to be super close. 'I have five friends whom I know that whatever happens will be there for me – if my career ends or if things go wrong. Even though they all live in different parts of the country, they are there for me and, better still, when they meet they all get on.'

Jane, on the other hand, says she doesn't like the term 'best friend' and prefers to have lots of friends who simply offer her different things, without putting a label on it. 'The concept of best friend is like being five years old,' she says. 'I couldn't pick a best friend. I have lots of friends. I like them all for different reasons. I have the friend in whom I would confide; the one I wouldn't confide in but would enjoy a fun night out with. I have lots of old school friends whom I still see.'

SHOULD OUR PARTNER BE OUR BEST FRIEND?

Do you tell your partner everything? Does he or she know your every secret? Would you describe them as your best friend? It's a funny one.

When you're committed to someone, you give each other everything – your heart, your loyalty, your time, your honesty. You shouldn't hide anything from each other, right? But do we hold some things back from our loved ones? Like things that we might want to get off our chest about them, but could ruffle their feathers?

Well, this is why we have a best friend to fall back on. They share a similar space in our hearts as our loved ones and are just as important to us, in a different way. Our other halves may listen to our woes, but with our very best friends we can open up and be totally honest about certain issues within our romantic relationships, such as sex problems or infidelity. Or any other tricky subject you know your other half will struggle to get their head around.

As much as Nadia adores Mark – and we know she worships the ground he walks on – she says her best mates are so important to her because they give her the chance to talk about things she can't discuss with her husband.

'I've got a best friend whom I can tell everything to,' she says. 'I think if your partner is your best friend, you're not having any sex! Talking to your best friend is different because there is some stuff that breaks the magic with your partner. I would talk to my friend about stuff that only another female friend would know all about.'

Coleen, on the other hand, thinks that when she's with a partner, she feels closest to them. 'I would say that my partner or husband would definitely be my best friend,' she says. 'I would tell him things that I wouldn't dream of telling my girlfriends or family. If something good happens for me, or really bad, the person I want to tell first, more than anyone, is my other half. He would totally feel my happiness or my sadness, and I always think of him first before phoning a friend.'

But there are some lines that she does draw with a partner. 'I don't share everything,' she concedes. 'Certainly I don't share the bathroom if I am in there! Some people are comfortable to do that; I'm not. I think some things should remain private and mysterious. But I share absolutely everything else.'

All that said, Coleen acknowledges that other friends do have a place in both her and any partner's life, admitting, 'You do need your girlfriends in your life and he needs his male friends to discuss other things.'

Unsurprisingly, Janet's view is more controversial. She says she doesn't believe in sharing everything with a partner. 'It's a very dangerous strategy. I have lied to all of them! Honesty is very, very overrated. There's not a lot to be said for honesty in a marriage.'

She explains that her relationships tend to shift over time. When she first meets someone, they are united in a strong friendship, which changes when they start to take things more seriously. 'I think I'm best friends with them before I live with them, before I have a relationship with them,' she says. 'I love the best-friend bit before, and when it's all over we'll go back to being best friends – about three months after break-up.'

She says that when they become intimate and a proper couple, she finds it uncomfortable to be as open as she was before. 'To be honest, I don't want my partner to know too much about me,' she says. 'I want them to know about one third. I want to be mysterious, I want to surprise them. And I don't want them to know all about me because I'm a bit like an iceberg. There's only one third above the waterline and two thirds going on down below!'

Janet adds that she fears that women who consider their husband their best friend are in danger of losing a bit of their identity. 'People who are in love with their partner and look to them as a confidant or best friend can find themselves getting so bound up that it's almost like they've been sucked in to occupy one half of their head and what you're about will always suffer.'

Nadia says she thinks a partner should be someone whom you love, but not be the one you share everything with. 'I've got a couple of friends who aren't married to the best of people and when we have chats, I say to them, "How can you put up with this? Why are you staying with them?" And they always reply, "Oh, but I love him." And I ask them, "Do you actually like him?" and they can't say it! You see, I want to be in love with my husband and I want to really like him. Those two things are important to me for a good relationship. But to make him my best friend as well is kind of too much for one relationship. We're asking for everything of it.'

Meanwhile, Gloria says that she thinks the foundation to any good relationship is having a strong friendship. 'It is so important to have that with your partner, especially when you are an older couple,' she says. 'Kindness and a sense of humour are important too, but the friendship part is terribly important – to know your partner and to know that even when the chips are down and the odds are against you, that you still like each other and can talk about everything. You need to be open.'

SHOULD YOU DITCH A MALE FRIEND WHEN YOU GET MARRIED?

We all know what some men can be like when we hang out with another man – easily threatened and reliably jealous. There are different ways to interpret this. Sometimes it seems sweet, because it suggests they love us so much they are scared of losing us. However, sometimes it can feel as if we are being regarded as their property.

In fairness, women are no different. If our man was spending a lot of time hanging out with an attractive female friend, we'd probably be wondering what was going on, too. It all comes down to that age-old debate about whether men and women can just be friends.

Having a circle of friends is important, so we get all points of view and understand how various kinds of people think. We need our girlfriends, our gay mates and the straight men in our lives too. So how would we feel if our boyfriend told us in no uncertain terms that we had to ditch our straight male mates if we were going to get married? Would we comply? Or would we ignore them?

'Well, being honest, I wouldn't like my husband to be going out with other women, even if they were just friends,' Gloria says. 'I wouldn't want that. No. I'm quite jealous at heart. I would be jealous of the time he might spend with another girl, for whatever reason.

Of course, there are business reasons, on both sides, for us to be with the opposite sex, which I do understand. But I'm not proud of the fact that I'm jealous, which I am, and I always say to Stephen, "Look if I didn't care and love you so much I wouldn't mind what you were doing or who you were with."

But what if Stephen dared to tell her she couldn't see her male friends? 'For a start, we do tend to meet friends together. I don't hang around with straight chaps,' she clarifies. 'I have a lot of gay friends, so he has nothing to worry about there. But if I was out with a former boyfriend I think he'd be anxious. And, in reverse, I wouldn't like it. However, having said that, friends are so important.'

Unsurprisingly, Janet is adamant that no partner will ever tell her who she can or can't be friends with. 'It's an absolute rubbish suggestion! I think that when you meet someone and you start a new relationship, you don't ditch all your friends, you don't edit people out. If they're your friends, they're your friends. If you love someone and they love you back, they should value the people you already know. Your friends are a reflection of yourself. I haven't ditched old boyfriends, definitely not.'

But is Janet content for her partner to carry on socialising with his close female friends? Is she ever worried that he might be lured away from her? Of course not, Janet is a live-and-let-live kind of woman who understands that no one has the right to wipe out someone else's history.

'My partner still sees his friends from ages ago; he had one visit him in the country recently,' she says, matter-of-factly. 'Your friends are your friends, even old girlfriends who he was seeing probably a half-century ago. It's good having old friends as they can have a good point of view about the life you're living now.'

Nadia agrees with Janet and thinks both partners should be able to maintain healthy and fruitful friendships with the opposite sex, though she can understand why some men and women, hurt by a cheating partner in the past, might be extra cautious in the future.

'I suppose if you had experiences of men cheating on you, you might be more careful and protective,' she says. 'However, in my case, with Mark, I just completely trust him so he can be friends with whoever he likes, which I know a lot of people think I'm stupid for thinking, but I really do. I actually actively encourage Mark to have female friends. One of my close friends has become a very close friend of his, and they go off and do things together without me and I love that. Because I think that this friend of mine is such a grounded person in so many ways. She's sort of cleverer than me, and Mark's cleverer than me, so they kind of feed each other on that. And then I'm much more fun than either of them so I feed them on that.'

Nadia says she has a very open and fearless relationship with Mark because she grew up in a happy family that wasn't rocked by infidelity.

'I think I am so trusting because my dad is very loyal,' she says. 'My mum and dad still hold hands. They've been together for over 50 years and to my knowledge neither has cheated. So I suppose I don't carry that fear. Who knows, if somebody had cheated on me, or my dad had been like that, I probably would be more worried.'

However, Nadia does admit that she might not be as open to Mark having close female pals if they had too much in common. 'I wonder sometimes how I would feel if when I'd met Mark and he had a really close, playful girlfriend who could ski and who liked *Star Wars* and all of that. Maybe I would be a bit uncomfortable with that. But I could hope I would push through it.'

WOULD YOU TELL YOUR FRIEND IF YOU DIDN'T TRUST THEIR PARTNER?

It's one of the worst situations to be in. Your best mate introduces you to her new man and, for some reason, you feel something's not right.

You don't know what it is, but you have a strong sense that something about this guy isn't right and you can see the relationship ending in tears. So what do you do? Do you tell your friend that she can do better? Or do you let her enjoy the time she has with the chap, wait for nature to take its course and make sure you're on hand to help pick up the pieces? It's a tough decision. People have to make their own mistakes, and it feels uncomfortable to interfere in other people's business. How would you feel if your friend chipped in and said, 'Look, I don't think he's right for you?'

Well, Saira is adamant that she would say something, because that's what real friends do. 'If you are my friend and I'm not sure about your partner, I will say something like, "I just need to let you know I don't like him but it won't affect our relationship and I will still hang out with you."'

Saira says that being a good friend means you have to be honest. 'I cherish my friendships. I would never want to lose a friend because I hadn't stepped up and said my piece,' she confesses. 'You can't be a true friend if you can't be honest. I'm very honest. In fact, all the Loose Women say I have no filter and they always tell me to be less direct. Even Nadia said to me, "God, you're a hard bitch."'

Coleen says she wouldn't feel comfortable wading in and informing her friend that the man she was seeing wasn't good enough. 'I wouldn't tell them directly and say, "I don't like the look of him, I don't trust him," because the problem with it is, if they're in love with them, it doesn't matter what you say to them. And then when we will tell her "somebody told me this about him" or "apparently he used to do that", she'll just say "he's with me now." And then your heart sinks as you realise she is totally oblivious to what is going on.'

The other fear, Coleen points out, is that the fella in question will find out that you're expressing doubts about him and he will try to phase you out of your friend's life. 'If you tell her, she's bound to tell him and he'll convince her not to like you any more. So I think as a good friend you might have suspicions, and if it does go pear shaped, you're there to help her get through it. But I don't think I would destroy her.'

Jane is an advocate for friends interfering if they think someone in their mate's life is not quite right. But, she suggests, you have to pick the right moment to do it. 'It's totally about timing because I think if a friend says to me, so-and-so has asked me out on a date and I know that they *are* a right "so-and-so" I'll say something, because at that early stage they haven't had a chance to fall in love.'

However, Jane understands that some people do change, and that just because a guy has had a bad relationship with one girlfriend that doesn't mean he will continue that behaviour with another. 'There are some people who have been one way with one person and they meet somebody else and they are not that way,' she says. 'So there's always that little thread of hope. I would probably say something if I was unsure about a friend's partner. But then who wants to be the person when your friend is in that besotted phase pouring a jug of cold water over everything that they're feeling.'

Jane says that if she saw 'signs of abuse or violence, or very controlling behaviour', she wouldn't hesitate to step into a friend's relationship.

'If I knew a friend's partner was cheating, I'd want to tell them, but I'd probably just send an anonymous letter or something!' she says. 'I'd want her to know, but the messenger always gets shot.'

If a friend asked for help, on the other hand, Jane would be only too happy to get involved, even if it meant having to roll her sleeves up and get slap bang in the middle of the action. 'There was a friend of mine who was really upset because her boyfriend had dumped her, and she said, "I think he's got another woman, but I don't know." So I went round to his flat, knocked, he tried to close the door so I put my foot in the way, and I said, "Why have you upset my friend?" and he said, "It just wasn't working, we weren't compatible." So I asked, "Is there no one else then?" And I could see this woman in the background. So I burst in and looked at her, and went, "You left my friend for her?! Don't ever contact my friend again, leave her alone."'

Gloria is a lot more reserved than the other women and admits that she would feel cautious about interfering too much in a friend's relationship unless they specifically asked her for advice.

'Well I know for a fact that the husband of somebody I know is having an affair,' she says. 'And I cannot bring myself to tell that person because it's so damning. It's a tough one, because on the one hand I want her to know that she's being taken for a ride, and yet on the other hand I don't want to strip away her life in one sentence.'

Gloria says it's harder for her to intervene when it comes to stepping into her children's relationships. 'When your grown-up kids start bringing home boyfriends/girlfriends, as a parent you have an opinion on what they are like,' she muses. 'But you have to be careful about what you say as there is a danger you could drive them away, if you start complaining about them and getting too vocal. I think in that scenario you have to let it play out. But then we have to ask ourselves – do we have the right to say to somebody, "He/she is not suitable for you?" To be honest, I don't think we can really judge!'

Kaye says that it is wise to consider the consequences of sharing your opinion about a partner with a friend before you say the words. 'I think you have to gauge whether they are ready to listen, or if they actually want to listen to you,' she says. 'You have to ask, are you doing it for you, so you feel like you have done the right thing? I think the best thing is to be there to pick up the pieces.'

IS IT GOOD TO HAVE BRUTALLY HONEST FRIENDS?

What do you look for in a friend? Loyalty, love, excitement? Yes, yes, yes to all of the above. But don't we all want honesty too? After all, if we're heading out on a girls' night and our make up looks smudged, wouldn't we want one of our mates to step in and tell us?

But can honesty go too far? Is there a line we shouldn't cross;

should we think twice before saying something that could potentially crush and destroy someone's self-esteem?

Jane says that she would like to think of herself as a very honest but diplomatic friend, but when push comes to shove she'd more than likely cave in and pretend to like something. 'If a friend asked me about a dress she wanted to buy that really didn't look good on her I'd probably say, "Oh, let's have a look at what else there is,"' she says. 'But if they're coming out of their bedroom and obviously they've decided this is what they want to wear, I'd just say, "You look lovely!"'

Jane admits that she doesn't think she could cope with a pal being too honest with her. 'If I had a friend who constantly criticised me, I think I'd probably go, "Do you know what, you're a bit hard work, mate! I think I'll find another friend!"'

Nadia says it can be hard sometimes to tell if a friend really wants advice or if they merely want someone to back up what they were already thinking.

'You can tell from the look in your friend's eyes whether they really want the truth,' she says. 'But I was having a conversation with a friend of mine recently on the phone so I wasn't getting proper eye contact. She asked me a question and I told her what I thought and she went, "Yes, or it could be...' and then I realised she'd already made up her mind and didn't need advice but just wanted a bit more confidence.'

However, Jane warns that there are certain occasions when we should be cautious about being a brutally honest friend. 'The worst one is when your friend says that she has split up with her boyfriend, and you go, "Oh thank God for that. I never liked him; what an idiot he was." Then a week later, they're back together!'

HAVE YOU STRUGGLED TO SHARE
A FRIEND'S BABY JOY?

Usually, when someone shares the news they are expecting a baby, we are thrilled for them. If they have been dreaming of starting a family, it's a really exciting time. But if, for one reason or another, you were finding it hard to have a baby, would you still be able to feel happiness for your mates who were having no trouble getting pregnant?

Saira, who struggled to have children during her thirties, says she found it hard to deal with when her friends announced that they were embarking on family life. 'I was 34 when Steve and I started to try and get pregnant and it just wasn't happening,' she reflects. 'By this time, all my friends were married; my brothers and sisters were married. They'd all had children, and Steve and I just couldn't conceive. I didn't want it to, but it got me down and depressed and just so upset and I couldn't be happy for people. God, it sounds terrible.'

In spite of her inner heartache, Saira would try her best to congratulate her friends on their happy news. 'Well, you kind of have to, don't you?' she concedes. 'You say "well done" but then I'd go home and be really upset and cry. I remember there was one Christmas when we saw a lot of pictures of our friends with their children and it broke my heart. Our friends didn't really know we were struggling; we would just put a brave face on it. But deep down I was so devastated and so we just took ourselves away for Christmas.'

Coleen says she sympathises with how Saira felt having to see all these happy families springing up, but she can also see how hard it can be on the couples who are pregnant and having to share their news with friends who might be struggling like Saira. In fact, she says she went through an experience with her sister Bernie that left her wracked with guilt.

'I remember when I got pregnant with Ciara; Bernie knew she was pregnant a couple of weeks before I found out,' she recalls. 'It was all going nicely and we were like, "Oh, we're going to be pregnant together!" and the babies were due to be born a couple of weeks apart and we were so excited. And then Bernie miscarried and she and her husband were devastated. I was too. But then it felt so hard for me to go to the scans because I felt so guilty.'

Luckily, Coleen's sister managed to deal with her feelings of loss so that she could still support her sister through this joyous time. 'Bless Bern, she would phone me every time and ask "How did it go?"' she says. 'But I'd feel so awkward. When Ciara was born, Bernie was the first one to turn up at the hospital and hold her and that made me cry. Bernie said, "I'm delighted for you. I wanted my own; I don't resent you having one."' But I felt awkward, almost guilty, that I was sailing through it.'

LOOSE LESSONS

- Remember, friends come in all shapes and sizes. Some are drinking pals, some are work friends and then there are the ones you'll confide in. It is always best to have a selection!

- Your partner can be your best friend, but don't isolate yourself from other friendships.

- If you are tempted to be honest with a friend about their partner, think about if it's actually what is best for them.

BAD FRIENDS

WOULD YOU HAVE SEX WITH A FRIEND'S BOYFRIEND AS REVENGE?

 If a friend did the dirty on you and, say, stole your fella, what would you do about it? Forgive and forget? Well, maybe. It happens! But if there was a moment that arose later down the line and that frenemy did something that really hacked you off, would you take your revenge like one of our Loose Women did and sleep with their man? Can you guess who...?

'I'm not proud of this, and it's very bad...' Coleen begins. 'But a long, long time ago, this girl had an affair with a boyfriend of mine. Me and the guy finished and this girl started dating him.'

Coleen stayed mates with the ex and even forged a friendship with the girl who had originally broken her heart! But, predictably, that relationship didn't last for long.

'We got to be friends, but then she said to me one day about "our" boyfriend straying, "The difference between you and me is, he wouldn't do it to me."'

The comment made Coleen's blood boil.

'I couldn't believe what I was hearing! So do you know what I did? Yes, I went and slept with my ex again that night, and the next day walked straight up to her and said, "He did." She was really upset and I did feel really bad. But she shouldn't have been so cocky with herself, so she only has herself to blame!'

DO WE TAKE ADVANTAGE
OF OUR GIRLFRIENDS?

Our female friends are so important to us. We can talk to them about all sorts of things, and rely on them to give us an honest opinion when we really need to. But is it easy to hold on to them? And have we ever been guilty of taking advantage of the friendship and cruelly ditching them when an attractive man appears on the scene? And what if a friend starts to bring us down? Should we cut them out of our lives, or should we put them on the back burner until they sort themselves out?

Coleen says that her mates are an essential part of her life and she tries really hard to ensure that they are all on the same page and keep in touch even when she's at her busiest. But she admits that there are times when we put friends through the wringer – not least when we start dating someone new, and all of sudden our best mate and confidante becomes old news!

'When you meet someone and you think you love them and that maybe this is the one, you do become wrapped up in them and you want to be with them every minute of the day,' she says. 'A good, understanding friend will think, "I'll wait and let her get this out of her system, she'll soon get bored and come back to me" or "He'll soon get on her nerves and she'll want to moan about him." Good friends accept that of one another. However, if the friend starts to feel jealous I don't think that's very healthy. But I do think it is important to not completely drop your friends, because they will definitely be with you for life!'

HAVE YOU EVER FELT OVERSHADOWED BY YOUR ATTRACTIVE FRIENDS?

Do you have any friends who are so strikingly beautiful that they turn heads wherever they go? And how does that make you feel when you go out together? Or what about that friend who is so outgoing and funny that everyone in the room immediately hangs on every word they say? It can be hard on your confidence if you feel overshadowed by a brilliant friend, but it's important to try not to let it get to you. After all, everyone has their hang-ups and their problems, as well as their most attractive features.

Saira knows only too well about feeling invisible. When she was at university she made friends with a fellow student whom she can only describe as 'absolutely stunning'. 'She had beautiful long, shiny dark hair, perfect teeth, big eyes,' she remembers. 'We all wanted to be her friend, which was great. And we'd go clubbing and stuff. She was actually really lovely as well, which was very annoying!'

As much as Saira enjoyed hanging out with the heavenly beauty, she and her girlfriends would get annoyed when all the boys in the student bar fixated on her and not them.

'We didn't get a look-in for months,' Saira says. 'And then it got to the point where one of the girls had organised a night out and said, "Oh, I didn't invite the pretty girl. We need a night off for us girls, let us go and enjoy ourselves. Otherwise we're never going to get a look-in, are we?!'

And so in order to help them grab a bit of the limelight, Saira and the girls would plan social engagements without 'pretty girl' in tow. 'Her prettiness was a bit of a curse for her in the end, because we ended up going out a lot without her,' she says. 'Looking back it was a bit mean – we didn't want to be like that. It was just she was so pretty.'

Kaye understands the situation that Saira found herself in, but reckons the way she and her friends dealt with their pretty friend was how most young people would – as they don't yet have the life experience and maturity to deal with it in the best way. 'You're still a bit unsure of yourself and you're self-conscious,' she says. 'But as you get older, it changes, doesn't it?'

Coleen can testify to that and says that she doesn't feel so insecure around beautiful women any more. 'Yes, it changes when you're older,' she confirms. 'Now, when I go out with my stunning nieces – who are in their twenties and thirties – I'm just dead proud.'

But then, Coleen is used to competing for attention, having been raised in a family of six sisters. And, like Saira, she and her sisters had one particular beauty to contend with who took all the attention away from the others. 'It was hell on earth with my sisters!' she laughs. 'There's six girls from the same family. Maureen was the one who everybody fancied, and you'd walk in a room and they'd all go, "Love your sister!" and we'd all say "Maureen". Everywhere we went it was Maureen, Maureen, Maureen. She didn't know it, which made her even more beautiful, and that was really annoying! We couldn't even say, "She's a vain old cow!"'

Kaye says that when she and Nadia used to go out when they were living together back in the day, she would feel invisible as madcap Nadia held court in bars!

'Going out and about with Nadia was a bit of a nightmare – she's so vivacious, she's so kind of out there and everyone would love her,' she recalls. 'She was like a honeypot, everybody was around her because she's flirty and I'd be sitting by the toilets somewhere. I don't think she particularly knew it either. And then I'd slink off at 10 o'clock, go home and watch *Newsnight*.'

IS IT OUR FAULT WHEN FRIENDSHIPS FIZZLE OUT?

How often do you spool through your pics on Facebook and come across some from a few years before featuring a few faces of friends who are no longer part of your life?

It's only natural for us to lose touch with people as we weave our way through life, work and relationships. Sometimes we have big bust-ups and we swear never to speak to certain people ever again. But often the explanation is far less dramatic. There are the friends who move away so you rarely get to see them. Sometimes you start a new job and meet a whole new bunch of folk and, as a result, lose touch with friends from your previous workplace, with whom you have less in common now.

To maintain all the friendships we form over the years is not easy and would no doubt take up so much time we'd have no time to do anything else. But are we being selfish when we let pals slip away? Should we make more of an effort to keep them close or is it inevitable that some people will disappear from our lives?

Janet has spoken about how she has met and befriended many people over her 70-plus years. However, during that time she has stuck by some and waved goodbye to others.

'I've got really close friends that I've had since I was 18,' she comments. 'We still go on holiday together and some of them have seen me through all four husbands. As you get older, you feel comfortable with certain people. There's only a certain number of close friends you can actually cope with – you're deluding yourself if you think you can handle more than a small handful. So you have a second circle of friends who you don't see so often, but who you get on with. But there is a finite number, so for me, it's one in, one out.'

However, Janet admits that the friends she dearly loves won't let her get away with being grouchy, so she has to work extra hard to ensure they stick by her. 'I've got friends who are tough with me,' she reveals. 'They might not like the way I behave and say, "Janet, you're being a complete ****." But if I want to remain friends with them then I modify my behaviour. I have to take it on the chin so I am prepared to accept that I'm horrible at times.'

Who'd have thought that feisty Janet would compromise and adjust her behaviour for others?! But don't let this make you think she's gone soft.

'I have "edited" friends out of my life because they became too demanding and it wasn't an equal friendship,' she declares. 'If someone expects you to be at their beck and call all the time and then when you are there they either fall asleep or ask you for money, well then they can **** off!'

'There was one I edited out because, the last time I saw her, I was having dinner with her and her partner, whom I really liked, and I looked round and she was asleep at the dinner table!' she recalls, still astonished. 'So I thought, "Right, I've got the message!" How do I dump them? Well, I just don't include them in anything.'

Janet says her best friends are those who live away from the media spotlight but have been by her side when life has been tough. 'I've been through some difficult patches in my life, where my friends have been very supportive and they've seen me at rock bottom,' she confides.

Janet thinks it's important to make sure you know who your real friends are, as opposed to people you like, but who are more like casual acquaintances. 'You have to differentiate between work mates and true friends, and a lot of people in Britain do not make that distinction, so when they lose their jobs or are made redundant they can feel very alone.'

But it's not just Janet who "edits" people out of her life. One of her mates actually did that to her – and she was shocked and saddened by her reason.

'I wrote a book years ago called *Life's Too F***ing Short*, and in it I said, "One of the things that you must do is to get rid of toxic friends that take more than they give and friends that just moan and are demanding." I also wrote, "When people are draining you – edit them out," and then it happened to me. One of my closest friends, a friend whom I'd known since I was 21, was supposed to come round for supper with me but didn't turn up. Instead, she sent a letter in which she said, "I'm sorry I don't want to see you any more – I just can't come." And she's never spoken to me since.'

The letter was a shock and left Janet upset and so she replied, keen to understand why her friend had said what she had. 'I wrote and begged her to remain my friend, but she still refused to speak to me,' she recalls. 'I later found out from her husband that part of the reason was that I made her feel a failure.'

She says their lack of contact breaks her heart as she still has photos of the pair of them on walks, going on holiday together, as they were going through various relationships at the same time. 'And now we're not friends,' she sighs.

While Janet understands that most friends support their mates if they are successful, she also sees why friends who aren't happy in themselves will find it hard to spend time with friends who make them feel even more insecure. 'Some friends feel threatened and you have to not rub it in their faces,' she explains. 'We've all got friends with less money.'

Gloria points out that her mum gave her some great advice. 'She said, "never surround yourself with negative people. Always positive. Otherwise you become negative yourself."

Saira says she finds it hard to maintain lots of friendships. 'One of my best friends I've known since I was 11, and I speak to her every day. Obviously that's really nice. But some of my other friends I've drifted away from. I have to say, I'm one of those people who needs to make more of an effort, but I'm just so tired and I make excuses and I'm not really that great. There's an understanding with me now. They think I won't turn up. But they don't dislike me for it.'

Coleen understands that sometimes circumstance will lead to you and your best mate not speaking for ages, but she believes that strong friendships will not be affected. 'If you've got a really solid relationship, you can not speak to your friend for six months but when you get together it's like you've never been apart,' she says. 'I've got a friend who lives in London and I live in Manchester; I think the last time I'd seen her was my fiftieth birthday, and then last year we went on holiday together and that was the first time we'd seen each other in two years. But it was like we'd never been apart. And then I've got a really best friend in Manchester who I see every day and it's a different relationship.'

Jane agrees that the strength of a friendship can alter depending on various factors. 'A lot of it's about location,' she explains. 'I've got some really good friends who live close to me, so for me it's more about spontaneity. If someone doesn't live near me and we try to make an arrangement, something always comes up so one of us ends up having to break it or whatever. Whereas if you can just text and go, "I'm going on a dog walk, shall I see you in the park?" that's kind of an easier way.'

Jane is so committed to her old mates that she will go to great lengths to see them, even if hubby Gary doesn't understand why. 'A very old friend of mine who I was at school with, and who I was with the night she met her husband, invited me to their thirtieth wedding-anniversary party in Worcester and I went,' she recalls. 'It was a Saturday night, so I got in the car and drove up there. Gary, who is a typical bloke and not as good at keeping up with his friends, was like, "Oh my God, you're driving all the way to Worcester and back?" But it was important to me because she was my friend and I had a wonderful time.'

CAN A FRIENDSHIP RUN OUT OF STEAM?

As we've discussed, close friendships can be just as important – sometimes even more so – as your relationships with your family and partner. But even so, just like a romantic liaison, friendships can run their course and there might come a point where you break up and go your separate ways. Can that split cause you as much heartache as breaking up with a partner?

Nadia believes that close friendships are as important and as serious as romantic ones. 'There's a lot of pressure to believe that a friend is for life. But I see it as like any other kind of relationship,' she says. 'In a way, you fall in love with your friends, you find things that you are both interested in, you have a laugh, you have fun doing things. But a friendship can run out of steam, just like a sexual relationship.'

Jane agrees that we shouldn't expect friends to be there for life, as it's inevitable that sometimes they will drift away. 'I don't believe that just because you have known them from ten, they will therefore be part of your life forever,' she says. 'They will be if you get on with them and keep that relationship going, but if not why should they?'

Coleen says that she has experienced the heartache of being dumped by a friend. And not just dumped, but 'ghosted' – phased out of someone's life without explanation or warning.

'I met this woman a few years ago and became instant friends. We just clicked,' she recalls. 'I loved having her around me. She brought great joy to my life. She was a carer and she worked hard. Then, two years down the line, she walked out of my life never to be seen again. At the time, it was like a break-up. I was devastated. I carried on texting her, trying to find out if I had done anything wrong and she got back to me and said that I hadn't done anything and that she had moved away.'

Nadia assures Coleen that the woman's actions were probably

driven by her own issues and nothing to do with her whatsoever. And she knows this because... she too has 'ghosted' a friend in the past! Not just anyone mind, but someone we all know very well.

'I am most ashamed to say this, but I have done that with friends,' she confesses. 'I did it to Kaye. But it was all about me. I was very insecure about whether I was good enough as a friend. I would think, "She's so clever" and I worked myself up. In the end we stopped talking – or I did – and we didn't speak for years. But then one day I just texted her and she came straight back in the next second and said, "You have always been my favourite person in the world, shall we meet up tomorrow?" and that was it and we were friends again.'

Kaye says that because she knew Nadia so well, she understood that her mate was going through a phase where she needed to retreat to the warm bosom of her family.

'I was confused to start with,' she recalls. 'I didn't understand why this was happening. She had withdrawn and I felt like I was left in limbo wondering why that was. I knew her well, and she is the kind of person who, when she's under pressure, will retreat to her core family group. I worked out she was retreating to the bunker. I was upset for sure, but I wasn't angry. When it was sorted we were straight back to being friends again.'

Gloria says she thinks strong friendships have to be nurtured and those will be the ones that will last longer even if you are not constantly around each other. 'One has to work at keeping in touch and feeding friendships. One particular relationship I had really stands out. When Caron was battling her seven-year cancer, one of my best friends Merrill said, "You can ring me day or night, four in the morning I don't care, I am there for you. You can speak to me." I never did call her at all hours in the dead of night. But I knew I could. Now that's a friendship.'

Back in Gloria's singing days, performing at a
Christmas Ball at City Hall in Belfast, aged 16.

At 18 years old, Gloria is at Old Fort Henry in
Ontario, Canada. She is sitting in the same seat
the Queen had occupied on a royal tour.

Gloria's wedding day to Stephen at Hever Castle,
Kent. They've been married for over 21 years.

Gloria with her daughter, Caron, on her
wedding day to Stephen, back in 1998.

Gloria with her husband Stephen,
dressed up for a Bollywood party!

Behind the scenes of *Strictly Come Dancing*. Gloria was a contestant
in the third series in 2005 and was partnered with Darren Bennett.

Jane, aged 6, at primary school in Oxford. Jane's mum had told her to put a hand over the hole in her tights, but she chose the wrong knee!

A recent photo of Jane on holiday in France.

Jane with her four-week-old daughter, Ellie, in Benidorm.

Jane with her beloved dog, Jasper.

Jane and Gary on their wedding day, on the 4th May 2002. They are with Gary's daughter, Lauren, and Jane's daughter, Ellie.

Saira with her dad, Jan Mohammed Khan; her mum, Hanifa Khan, and her sister, Sajdah. Saira is at the front in the striped dress. This was taken in 1975, a few days before Saira's parents flew back to Pakistan to visit their family.

Saira and Steve about to go out for a date night.

Saira with her son, Zac, and daughter, Amara.

Saira with her mum, Hanifa, and her daughter, Amara. Three generations of women: Hanifa was born in Kashmir, Saira was born in Nottingham and Amara was born in Karachi, Pakistan, and adopted from the Edi foundation.

Saira and her daughter Amara appeared together on the show in September 2018, telling the story of Amara's adoption. Saira sees her infertility as a blessing as it brought Amara into her life. She says Amara is everything she hoped a daughter could be.

LOOSE LESSONS

- It's natural to sometimes feel overshadowed by more attractive friends, but remember you have your own wonderful qualities and it doesn't always pay to be beautiful!

- Over the years we move in and out of various friendships and we should feel comfortable acknowledging that some friendships will come to a natural end.

- Don't ever ghost a mate. Being suddenly ditched by a good friend can be heartbreaking.

PART 5
FAMILY AFFAIRS

'You can choose your friends, but you can't choose your family,' the old saying goes. Which means if you don't get on with them, you're stuck. The family dynamic is a funny one. Siblings may vie for attention, mums and dads might drift in and out of love; they may fall out with their kids. And then when boyfriends and girlfriends or step-parents are thrown into the mix, there is plenty of opportunity for disagreements or long-held resentment to bubble up to the surface. Here, our Loose Women share with us their family experiences and how they have coped during the best and worst times.

YOUR FAMILY AND THEIRS

MEETING THE PARENTS

Introducing your new partner to your parents is nerve wracking for sure. Not only do you pray that they will like them but you also hope that they won't embarrass you in the process!

Having been brought up Muslim, Saira knew that introducing her white, atheist boyfriend Steve to her mum was going to be no walk in the park. In fact, for the previous four years, she had been living a lie and hadn't told her mum that Steve was even in the picture, because having boyfriends was frowned upon.

However, when Steve popped the question, Saira knew it was time to come clean to her mother. 'I phoned my brothers and sisters up, knowing what my mum is like, and said, "I'm coming down with Steve, obviously don't say anything, but make sure she is on her best behaviour, make sure she looks all right."

'So we're driving up to the house, and Steve's looking around, but when we open the door to the garden, we find my mum sitting there on the doorstep crouched down with a hubble bubble pipe and a scarf wrapped round her neck. Steve looked at me and went, "Who's that?" "That's my mum," I said. Then she got up and started talking to me in my language and didn't say hello to Steve in English. Steve whispered to me, "What's she saying?" I told him, "She said your suit looks really nice," but what she was really saying was, "Of all the men you could have picked, have you got to choose one with a bald head and a big nose?" Then she broke into this traditional wailing, saying, "Oh my God, she's married a white man, what shame you bring on my family." I assured Steve that it was just for show, and she had to be seen to be disapproving, otherwise people wouldn't accept it. He said, "Have I just got to sit through it?" and I said, "Yeah, just sit through it.'"

Eventually, Saira's mum let him into the house and has grown to love Steve so much that now she constantly warns Saira that "If you ever leave Steve, I will kill you!"

Coleen's first encounter with her mother-in-law wasn't quite as dramatic as Steve's. 'When I was 21, I met my Shane's mother for the first time and I have to admit it was a bit daunting. She was a lovely, warm Irish woman and we got on great. But then Shane said to her that we were planning on moving in together. When Shane left the room for a moment, she leaned over and said, "He'll be home in six weeks." And I joked, "Yeah, probably, with my cooking!"'

Even though her marriage to Shane didn't last, she says that she has maintained a healthy relationship with her mother-in-law and that, "To this day I love her to pieces."

Jane reveals that she'd always thought that hubby Gary's first meeting with her mum had gone without incident, and only discovered years down the line about the cocky impression he had made on her mother. 'The first day he met my mum, he came for lunch at her house,' she recounts. 'He arrived in his Porsche and said to my mum, "This looks like a dodgy area, can I move your car so I can park mine in your space?"'

In spite of this initial encounter, Gary has proved to be a very devoted son-in-law, and even volunteered to stay behind from a family holiday to look after his mother-in-law when she broke her hip.

IS YOUR RELATIONSHIP DOOMED IF YOUR FAMILY DON'T LIKE YOUR PARTNER?

As we've seen, that first meeting between your parents and a new partner can be pretty daunting. In most cases, if he's a good guy, parents will usually welcome their future son-in-law with open arms – albeit it after a carefully studied trial period! But what if mum and dad take an instant dislike to your man? Do you ditch him, because your parents' opinions are important to you, or do you stand by your own judgement and risk damaging your relationship with them in the long run?

Gloria says parents have to be careful when it comes to meeting and approving their child's new man or woman. 'It's a fine line,' she says. 'If you push your children away by saying, "I don't like this person and I never want them in my house," then you run the risk of losing your children and any relationship with possible future grandchildren. I was lucky. In my case, Caron was bliss. There was nobody I didn't like and when she met her husband, Russ, I knew he'd look after her.'

However, while her relationship with her children's partners proved happy, she had a different experience when she introduced her first husband, Don, to her parents. Growing up in Northern Ireland with its religious divide was tough and fraught with prejudice. So when Gloria, who was brought up Protestant, got engaged to an English Catholic man, her strict father found himself in a rather tricky dilemma.

'When I introduced my dad to Don, he was very nice to him even though there was this religious difference hanging in the air,' she recalls. 'However, my father was a very principled man and told me that if I married Don he would not attend the wedding. Nor would he let my mother attend. Even though I wanted her to come, she wouldn't have gone against her husband in those days. However, my father did allow my sister and my brother to go.'

Even though she was heartbroken by her father's decision not to attend the wedding, Gloria says she was touched when her father still gave Don the seal of approval. 'My dad said to Don, "If you decide to get married I can't approve because you are a Catholic, but I do promise that you'll be like a son to me the day you get married." The best thing is, he stuck to that, so I admired him for it – he worked out how to deal with it and they got on famously.'

NIGHTMARE MOTHERS-IN-LAW

There's an old saying that you shouldn't trust a man who doesn't love his mother. And while there's probably something in this, the slightly annoying flip side comes when his mum has made his life to date super easy by always cooking and cleaning for him. And when the going gets tough, he pops off back home and gets mummy to sort his life out. It's not too bad if your man is actually capable of doing things for himself too, but if he often prioritises his dear old mum over you or – worse – his mum is an overbearing busybody intent on wrecking your relationship, it can cause serious problems.

As expected, Nadia has a well-trained husband who is not only devoted to his mum but equally so with his wife. 'Mark's brilliant. He treats both of us beautifully,' she says. 'He is a very good son and a very good husband.'

However, she does confide that – before Mark – she had a boyfriend whose mother was difficult. Looking back, Nadia reckons she was the kind of mum who didn't like the idea of someone stealing her baby! 'We'd always have a meal the night before she went off and every time he left the room, she'd say, "When are you going to leave him? Can't you see how unhappy he is?"'

LOOSE LESSONS

- Mothers-in-law are not always as scary as you might think. You may actually find they become a very good friend.

- Your mum might initially take issue with your partner, but give it some time and let them build a better relationship.

- Remember, if a mother-in-law is tough, it's not always that she is mad at you, it might be that she is used to worrying about her child.

FAMILY RELATIONSHIPS

DEALING WITH A DIFFICULT CHILDHOOD AS AN ADULT

Adverts, Instagram, Facebook, those cheesy stock snaps you find in picture frames in shops – everywhere you look it seems you see happy, smiley families living their best lives. It's just so heart-warming to look at – unless, of course, your family life is nothing like that!

Sometimes siblings fall out, or mums and dads aren't as loving as you'd want them to be. But as we get older, those of us not living within a picture-perfect family have to learn how to deal with those unhappy surroundings and try to forge a better life for ourselves in the future. Janet grew up with her mum Cherry, dad Stanley and sister Pat in a small house in Fulham, west London, which was divided into two flats. It wasn't exactly one of the closest of family units and there was little in the way of familial warmth.

'We didn't speak at mealtimes, there was no chat,' she recalls soberly. 'There were loads and loads of rules. And the first rule that I can remember now is, every time we went on holiday, that business of packing the suitcase the night before and having it in the hall by 5am! Then you all got in the car and drove for miles! And then we'd have a cup of tea in a lay-by, made with a Primus stove.'

She remembers that her father liked things a certain way. Sometimes he would make her mum put on a clean apron to serve tea at six o'clock, and when they'd go away for the weekend, her mother would wear a string of pearls and an apron while having a picnic on a beach! The pictures they took on these occasions suggested to the world that they were a family living the high life, but the truth was they had no money whatsoever.

When she was 18, Janet got engaged before hastily calling off the wedding and then ran away from home and moved in with another man, whom she would later marry. Her mother was furious. 'She said to me that she was embarrassed by what I had done,' Janet recalls. 'She thought my behaviour was just terrible and she couldn't hold her head up in the street because of how I had been behaving.'

But there was something else that caused a wedge between mother and daughter, which Janet believes was to do with their general mistrust of each other. When her father died, Janet and her sister discovered that her mother had in fact been married to another man, something she had kept secret for years. 'I feel I didn't know my mother,' she explains. 'We had this strange relationship. She was secretive, but it was the 1950s and that's what people were like. But it's weird that when I was well known and working lots on the telly she must have been really anxious that the truth would have come out.'

But long before that revelation took place, Janet found it hard to relate to her mother and vice versa. To start with, it seemed crystal clear that her mother had developed a stronger bond with Janet's younger sister and subsequently would take her side in various matters, which led Janet and her sister to endure a very antagonistic relationship up until the death of their parents.

Even though she didn't really get on with her mother, Janet did come to understand why she might have been so angry and resentful all the time. Growing up poor in Wales, Janet's mother had been forced to go out to work at the age of 14 when her father stopped working at the local quarry. 'I can understand the resentment that must have built up inside of her over the years because she was highly intelligent and very gregarious,' Janet says. 'There are elements of my personality that I get from her.'

Her father, however, barely expressed any emotions. 'My father didn't show affection. He just talked to us, but didn't really say anything,' she remembers. 'I think he was a bit sad that the war had ended! He was no longer in the army where he had had lots of mates and found himself at home with only these two women and my mother to boss about.'

A strict and regimental man, Janet's father was something of a cold fish who put the fear of God into Janet. 'I would never cross him,' she says. 'But he would never hit me. He wasn't a jolly man. I never got cuddles. I think he was proud of me but he wasn't demonstrative.'

While he may not have shown warmth, he appeared to gravitate more to Janet than her sister. 'He was an engineer who had started off as an electrician and he was very ambitious for me,' she says. 'He used to take me to football and speedway and all those things. He used to make models with me as a child. So he projected onto me what he wanted to do.'

It was when her father and then mother died that the frosty relationship with her sister began to thaw. 'We'd already started to get close to each other after the death of our father,' she remembers. 'But it was definitely after the death of our mother that my sister and I got closer because our mother wasn't there to drive a wedge between us.'

However, their newfound alliance was cruelly cut short when her sister Pat was diagnosed first with lung cancer then brain cancer. 'Because there was little chance of recovery, Pat couldn't get the treatment on the NHS, so I supported her and paid for some of her treatment – anything to prolong her life. But to the end I think we were still arguing – we just did.'

Reflecting on her old family life (which is fully documented in her best-seller *Baggage*), Janet understands now that – in spite of the divisions – the unconditional love and loyalty she had for her family emerged in her sister's time of need. 'When the chips are down,' she says, 'all the acrimony and bitterness disappears. I didn't think twice and it gave her a few extra months of life.'

SIBLING RIVALRY

Are you an only child who longed for a brother or sister to join you as a playmate and partner in crime, having your back when you needed it? Perhaps you're lucky enough to be in a close-knit family with siblings who are also friends. Or maybe you grew up competing with your brothers and sisters for your parents' attention... Here, our Loose Ladies discuss how sometimes having a sibling can make life feel somewhat difficult!

Coleen had six sisters, which made her early life fairly hectic! But as the youngest, she was never part of the major fallouts. Instead she merely observed them as they'd 'rip Carmen rollers out of each other's hair'. However, as she got older, Coleen began to compete with her five sisters in trying to land boyfriends. 'I went out with a guy for two years and then, straight after me, Bernie went out with him for two years,' she recalls. 'It was awkward, especially when she would say, "Oh, he does this" and I'm like, "I know!" But in actual fact, me and Bernie didn't fall out over that because to me, well, no man is worth losing my sister over.'

Janet says that her relationship with her sister was troublesome from the moment Pat was born. 'I was outraged when she was born. How dare my mum have another child? I was forced to share a room with her and that was the worst thing that could have happened. So I drew a line down the middle of it, and I said, "Cross that and you're dead.'

Janet says she felt like her parents had their own preferred daughters . 'My sister was much more nice and smiley than me, so obviously my mother took her side, and my dad took mine in all family arguments, and I think that does happen when you have two children and two parents,' she reflects. 'It's not a good combo. When my sister arrived on the scene, we were so different, I just couldn't believe she had the same parents as me. So basically I think they picked up the wrong baby at the hospital. I was the brainy one but she had the curly hair! I hated her for having lovely curly hair and also because she was smiley.'

The dynamic within their relationship changed when their father passed on. 'Then my sister and I both had to contend with my mother,' she says. 'We got on really well until my sister ran away from home when she was 13 and took my savings book. Which had £25 in it.'

While Janet and Coleen had their fair share of drama with their sisters, Nadia says she had it pretty easy with hers. 'I'm the middle child and I love it,' she gushes. 'A lot of people say it's difficult being the middle child, but I think it's great because my older sister used to get all the responsibility, and my younger sister was completely spoilt. I was just in the middle doing what I wanted. So if I had the choice, I would always be the middle child.'

HAVE YOU EVER HAD TO
FIX A FAMILY FEUD?

Family dynamics can be a nightmare to contend with. Even if everyone gets along brilliantly most of the time, a bust-up or indiscretion, or the revelation of a deep, dark family secret can cause divisions and reopen old wounds or stoke new resentments. In cases like these, who should be responsible for healing the rift? If those involved don't seem to be in a hurry to sort it out and make amends, should you wade in and act as the peacemaker? How can you avoid getting dragged into disagreements and remain neutral?

Jane says trying to unite a warring family can be a very tough task to take on. 'It's tricky, isn't it? It depends on the reasons behind it; there are two sides to every story,' she says. 'And then you always face that dilemma of whether you take sides or try and take a steady course down the middle.'

Jane says that when she was younger, she discovered that there was a feud raging in her family that she hadn't known anything about. 'I met a guy through work, a gay guy, we hit it off, we got on brilliantly and we moved into a flat together,' she remembers. 'We went on holiday together to Key West. One day when he was writing his postcards, I noticed that he had written down Nana George and I said,

"That's funny, my grandma's surname is George" and he said, 'It's a very common name in Wales.'"

'When we got back home, my flatmate went to see his mum, and then he rang me and asked, "Is your grandma called Mary-Ann?" I said she was and he went, "Oh my God, we're cousins!" After looking through some photo albums, we discovered his grandfather and my grandmother were siblings, and we saw this cute picture of my mum and his mum when they were ten. It turns out our grandparents had had a massive argument, the family was divided and nobody had spoken to anybody for decades, which meant our mums hadn't spoken for years.'

So what happened next?

'Shortly afterwards, we went down to Wales, got his mum and my mum back together, did the picture again of when they were 10, it was amazing! No one ever knew what the feud was about, and yet 50 years later there were still repercussions. You have to ask, why?'

While Jane's tale had a happy ending, she concedes that sometimes family rifts can be so devastating that there is little hope of reuniting the family. 'There are some situations where it is untenable; you have to make a break,' she reasons. 'But otherwise you just talk about it, because of the impact on the children. When the wider family breaks up, it's not good.'

CAN OUR FATHERS' PARENTING SKILLS IMPACT ON OUR LIVES?

The relationship between a father and his little girl can be more complicated than the bond between mother and daughter. Some dads will protectively dote on their daughters and treat them like a little princess, spoiling them rotten and making sure they live a safe, happy and comfortable existence. Other dads, however, express their love by trying to teach their children some tough life lessons, to equip them to deal with difficulties in later life. But while these fathers may be simply trying their best to ensure their girls grow up to be independent and fierce young women, does their sometimes bullish behaviour impact on their daughters' subsequent parenting skills?

Saira thinks so. When she watches the incredibly strong bond between her hubby Steve and their adopted daughter Amara, her heart bursts with joy as she sees it as the most beautiful, intense father-daughter relationship. But as pleasurable as it is to her, it saddens her too because it reminds her of her fractured relationship with her own father.

'Watching Steve and Amara just makes me realise I didn't have that kind of bond with my dad,' she reminisces. 'And it's not because he didn't want it, he just couldn't show it.'

Saira explains that her father was an immigrant from Kashmir, Pakistan, who came to the UK with her mum and moved to a small town called Long Eaton in Derbyshire. 'I think my dad chose it because he quite liked the British way and wanted to integrate,' she says. 'I was allowed to do sport and my brothers were allowed to play football – and the fact that he let me go to university at 18 is a testament to his desire for integration.'

Although she never heard her parents talk about religion, she's sure 'it would have killed my father that I married a white guy who wasn't a Muslim.'

In later years, Saira's mum told her that before she was born her dad had been an alcoholic and doctors had said to him that he would die if he didn't stop drinking.

'So he just stopped, and as a consequence of that happening all the guilt, all the shame, all the stuff he felt bad about himself was sort of put on to me,' Saira says. 'He was really strict, nothing was ever good enough, he had really high standards that I could never achieve. I always felt that I was failing, but on the upside it made me the person I am today. I'm pretty strong, I'm ambitious, I've been successful in parts of my life.'

When she became a parent, she realised she was repeating her father's behaviour with her own children. 'My husband said to me, "There were moments with the kids' homework, you'd say, 'Why are you doing that? Put more effort in!'" But that was all I knew because I thought that's what you did to become successful.'

Worried about her parenting methods, she sought counselling, which helped her to deal with a lot of the issues floating around in her head. 'The biggest thing I've found by actually talking to somebody else is that while acknowledging I love my dad, there were things that my dad did that were wrong,' she reflects. 'There were moments when I was a child when I would say, "Dad, why are you doing this to us?" But at the same time, I'd be like, "You're my dad and I really love you, you've done everything for us," so it was very complex.'

Coleen says her relationship with her father was tough. While she explains that she and her siblings had a good relationship with him and that he was a great listener, he was also incredibly strict. She says that her father's heavy-handed treatment of her and her older sisters most definitely made an impact on her life. 'Right from when we were children, all the way up to when he got ill, and couldn't be there any more, our father was very controlling of my eldest sisters,' she says. 'He was a very strong force in our lives; he was very strict. One thing that stands out in my mind – I must have only been four or five – Linda and Bernie were having a fight and dad walked in and I remember him saying, "Because of you two, I'm going to have to smack her now as well" and I got a battering. I always remember it wasn't the hurt or the sting of the hit, it was just that it felt so unfair and I think it just stayed with me.'

Unlike Saira, Coleen didn't repeat the behaviour she had experienced growing up. On the contrary, she was adamant that would never treat her children in the same way. 'When I became a parent, I remember thinking, "I don't want to do anything to my children that isn't fair." That doesn't mean that I let them get away with murder, but I would explain to them why they were grounded or being told off – I wouldn't just go, "Because I'm the adult and children should be seen and not heard", which is what we got all the time.'

DO YOU SUFFER FROM DAUGHTER GUILT?

From the beginning, our mums make sure we are happy, well fed and never wanting for anything. And then what do we do? We up and leave home, become independent women and lose ourselves in careers and relationships, ultimately leaving them behind. Some of us might move many miles away from them. So if, in the course of our busy daily lives, we find we don't see our mums very often, should we feel guilty about that? Or is it just a rite of passage we all go through? After all, if we have become mums ourselves, our time and attention may be taken up with our own kids. While our love for our mums doesn't falter, if we're honest with ourselves, do we always show it?

Jane makes sure she catches up with her mum regularly, but – as she explains – it's easy as her mother lives just a stone's throw away, so she can drop by whenever she likes.

'My mum lives literally two roads away, so proximity wise, it's great and if I take the dog for a walk I can pop in for a cup of tea,' she says. 'Every Sunday is sacrosanct; everybody's there for Sunday lunch – kids, boyfriends, dogs, everyone all together.'

However, even though Jane's mum is getting on and loves catching up with her nearest and dearest, she's also carved out a very busy life for herself so that she's not just sitting at home waiting for friends and family to come a-calling.

'My mum's very independent,' Jane explains. 'She lives on her own, so there are days when I sort of think, "Oh you know, maybe I should pop in," but she's always doing something. She keeps herself busy. She works as a guide in Westminster Abbey and so she has a very active life and I think she likes the fact that I have an active life.'

However, reflecting on her relationship with her daughter Ellie, Jane says that she has started to notice some changes over the past few years as Ellie has grown up. 'For a long time it was just her and me, when I was a single mum,' Jane recalls. 'She's now working, she's really busy and every so often I will think, "Oh, I've not heard from her for three or four days," so I sort of make this tentative phone call – "Hi, it's mum..." and she'll say, 'Yeah, yeah, yeah – sorry, but I'm really busy, mum." It's like the roles are reversed a bit.'

Saira is happy to say that her relationship with her mother is incredibly strong, but admits that she does experience feelings of guilt from time to time, especially in the wake of the death of her father.

'After my dad died at 60 of a sudden heart attack, mum moved in with my younger brother in Nottingham,' she explains. 'And although she's got the family round her, she still feels lonely sometimes.'

Because of this, Saira decided to make an extra effort to spend more quality time with her mum and ditched a family holiday to have some essential one-on-one time with her. 'A while ago, Steve and I were going to go away on a little trip somewhere and I actually turned round to him and said, "Steve, you go away with the kids, I want to spend a whole week where there's just me and my mum."'

While it was a massive sacrifice to be apart from her husband and kids, Saira understood that being with her mother was precious and she wanted to ensure that they enjoyed their time together without any interruptions.

'I thought to myself, I don't want to look back on life and think every time she phoned me up I was just too busy, I'm working, I'm doing this,' she explains. 'So I took a week off, gave all my jobs up and spent a week with her. We went for a manicure, a massage and out for high tea. I spent the best week of my life.'

During their time together, Saira says she sensed that her mother was experiencing feelings of extreme loneliness, which she was trying to keep hidden. 'She was feeling lonely and I could feel it – even though she didn't tell me,' she says. 'I could just tell through her actions, through her lack of conversation. I thought, "My mum needs me right now," and we had such a lovely bonding time together.'

Gloria says that she always had a strong relationship with her mother and explains that they remained very close as they got older. 'I know people who have said that their parents never told them they loved them or hugged them,' she says. 'But I came from a very tactile, huggy family. If I'd gone to bed without kissing my mum and dad goodnight they would have thought that there was something really wrong. And when I visited them after I was married, my mum would stand at the door till I was absolutely out of sight. She was so warm and so funny, and fantastic. She was a wonderful mother.'

IS IT OK TO ADMIT YOU BEGRUDGE CARING FOR YOUR ELDERLY PARENTS?

One of the harshest aspects of growing old is watching our parents get frailer and sadly pass on. No matter how strong and independent we are, watching our parents fade away is one of the cruellest and most heartbreaking things anyone can experience. In the summer of 2017, Loose Woman Kaye posted online an emotional video about her poorly mum, who had been recovering in hospital after a stroke. In it, she asked the question, 'Why is it that we don't openly talk about our parents getting older and frailer?' The level of response she received was astonishing.

'Mum was going through a bad time,' Kaye says, referring to the point in time when she recorded the emotive clip that went viral. 'We'd only just lost my dad in February, whom she had looked after incredibly for three years. And then she had had a stroke. The family all tried to help her but she was the absolute mainstay.'

Kaye decided to post the clip because, as she sat with her mum in the hospital, it suddenly dawned on her that we never really prepare ourselves for the gradual decline of a parent. 'We talk a lot about parenthood and we joke that you don't get a manual for kids but there isn't a manual for this, either. I never saw this bit coming and I kind of feel a bit of a fool for that to be honest.'

She says that she found herself constantly fielding suggestions from friends who insisted she should take her mum out and about to various places. But, as Kaye explains, her mum was not someone who would be shunted around willy-nilly. 'My mum wasn't going to do that, I can't make my mum do anything because she is an independent person,' she says. 'She may have been a bit more frail but I couldn't just pick her up and put her where it suited me because that wasn't acceptable.'

During her mother's spell in hospital, she questioned whether or not she was selfish to think that she didn't have to visit her mother every single day. 'It's like, what are you allowed to do?' she muses. 'Are you allowed to take some time for yourself? Are you allowed to feel, actually, I don't want to go to the hospital today, or is that just a horrible thing to consider? I don't know.' Tough questions indeed, but ones many of us have pondered at some point.

Kaye lost her mother in 2018, and her death was devastating, but she was able to look back with warmth. 'I was blessed,' she says. 'I had the best parents, the most wonderful parents. I knew I was loved and I loved them. But we also need to talk about the way we are now, and to tell people when we are struggling.'

Coleen feels for Kaye, as it was very hard for her and her sisters to watch their mother deteriorate with Alzheimer's. Although for the first couple of years, her mum was still active and alert they were eventually forced to make the tough decision to give her 24/7 care.

Coleen admits that when her mother's health deteriorated dramatically, it became so heartbreaking to realise that sometimes she didn't want to keep visiting. 'When she got to the stage where she didn't know any of us, there was that awful moment when I couldn't bear seeing her like that,' she recalls. 'I just couldn't; it broke my heart every single day. So there were mornings when I'd wake up and think, "I don't want to go today. I don't want to see her." One part of you goes, "Well, you don't have to because she doesn't know who you are;

she'll never know." But then that child guilt kicks in – "She's my mum, I have to go."'

While her mind was everywhere during this time, Coleen says that she and her sisters were helped greatly by the Alzheimer's Society, who were on hand to give advice. 'We could phone them at any time and they knew what we were going through because they had been there too.' All I needed was someone to say that it was OK I felt like that, just to listen and not judge and say, "Why don't you do this?"'

LOOSE LESSONS

- Not everyone grows up within a happy family, but as you get older and gain experience things may change and relationships may improve. Things can get better.

- Of course we feel guilt towards our parents from time to time, but just make sure that you check in with them as much as you can and keep them involved in your life.

- Watching our parents get older and more frail is hard, and it is OK to sometimes think we don't want to see them going through tough times. This doesn't make us bad people.

THE NEXT GENERATION

ARE YOU TOO OLD TO BECOME A MUM OR DAD?

When an older man fathers a child, it doesn't seem to be a big deal. TV chef Gregg Wallace had his third child aged 54, and, in 2016, old rocker Ronnie Wood had twins at 68. However, women trying to have a child after 40 often find themselves under fire – from those who think women don't take their fertility seriously, or who believe it's a woman's 'responsibility' to start a family earlier.

Of course, it's largely up to the individual as to when and if they want to have children. Issues of fertility aside, is there an age that's 'too old' to become a mum? So long as the child is cared for and loved, does it matter how old its mum or dad is?

Nadia thinks older men in particular need to know when to draw the line. 'I think at a certain age you've got to stop,' she says. 'You see all these ageing rock stars, and they've already had eight, and you think, "Come on!"'

Saira says that she's not sure there should be a cut-off time to become a mum, and even admits she's still up for adding little ones to her brood. 'I'm in my late forties, perimenopausal and, I tell you, I don't know what's wrong with my hormones, but every time I see a baby I think, "I'm going have another one; I could have another one," and I'm literally staring at it.'

Saira knows she's unlikely to have a baby naturally. 'I would adopt. Amara's adopted, so I have been through the adoption process.'

However, she will still have to persuade Steve that it's a good idea. 'I have said to my husband, "Do you think we could have another baby?" And his answer is, "No, absolutely not, two is enough, that's it." And now I just keep niggling at him.'

'Often we don't think enough about very young people when they are having babies,' Nadia says. 'Mark had his first child at 22 and it was incredibly difficult. I was late – 38 and 42 for both my children. If I'd had them in my twenties or even my early thirties, I wouldn't be as good a mum as I am now.'

DO YOU TAKE ADVANTAGE OF GRANDPARENTS?

When your children are young, having parents around who are willing and able to lend a hand can be a godsend. But where should we draw the line with asking for their help? Is it OK to ask them to babysit on a regular basis, or can taking care of an energetic young child become an unwanted burden when they should be enjoying the freedom that retirement brings?

Grandmother to more than ten kids, Gloria says that she thinks most grandparents would be happy to oblige and babysit the kids from time to time. 'For the majority of grandparents, it's a real privilege,' she says. 'You love your grandchildren; they change your life. So I'd be the first in the queue if their parents asked would you like to come on holidays and help out. I really would.'

However, Gloria says it's important that parents are honest with the grandparents and explain why they need them to look after the children. 'Some years back, I wrote a book on grandparenting,' she recalls. 'I did a lot of research on it and I think what happens is – particularly when your daughter says, "Look, mum, we won't be able to afford childcare so will you have the baby? – you say, "Yes!' because you're so keen to take the baby on board. However, sometimes your kids think you are at their beck and call, but we grandparents might not want or be able to give them all our time. Sometimes, if a grandparent feels lumbered with the children, resentment sets in because they think, "This is my time. I'm retired now."'

Nadia thinks some grandparents must feel a certain pressure to take on their grandkids because they worry that if they refuse and kick up a fuss they risk not seeing them at all or very little. 'A lot of grandparents get fearful that if they try and put a boundary in place, they are going to alienate their child,' Nadia says.

However, she realises now that she did take advantage of her parents when Maddie and Kiki were born. 'My mum and dad lived next door, which meant it was easy to call upon them to help out with the kids,' she says. 'And when you have a newborn you are so excited and giddy that you think everyone is on the same giddy page. I think I fell foul of that.'

Nadia says that she now thinks her mother tried to highlight the stark realities of being a mum. 'When I look back over it, my mum gave me so many different warnings that being a mum wasn't all it was cracked up to be,' she says. 'She once said to me, "Motherhood is waking up every day, going 'Please God, not another day'." That was another clue that perhaps she wasn't keen to take on grandparenting duties! In my mind, I just thought she was going to love having my children all the time. It wasn't until years later, when my sister let drop that my mum had said something about babysitting, that I knew it hadn't been as much of a pleasure as I had thought. And I was so shocked.'

She remembers, 'When Maddie was small and I had really early calls for this morning show, I would go around the back garden of my parents' house with my child, open the back door, go into my mum's room and put her into the bed. I think I might have crossed the line but I didn't realise that at the time.'

Later, her mum confided to Nadia that being a grandparent didn't sit well with her. 'My mum said to me, "If one more person asks me if I'm pleased to be a grandparent, I can't be held responsible for what I do!"' she laughs. 'She didn't want to do anything! But of course, in the end she did loads and I couldn't have carried on without her. But it's your right as a grandparent to say no. My mother-in-law is a bad grandma because she's so badly behaved! She'll come for a sleepover and only want to eat crisps and drink fizzy drinks, and I can hear Kiki telling her off!'

Coleen says when she became a grandmother to Shane Jr's daughter Amelia she was thrilled because she got to get involved. 'I felt amazing. We were all in tears when she was born. She was absolutely stunning and beautifully pink with a mop of black hair. She was a mix of her mummy and daddy. She had Shane Jr's eyes and nose, and her mum's lips and cheeks. She was gorgeous.'

When she saw her son Shane Jr hold the baby in his arms, Coleen melted. 'It was such an emotional time and I really got what the big deal is about becoming a grandparent. It was my baby holding his baby, and it was overwhelming. I felt so proud of him.'

As soon as she got her head around the shock of becoming a gran, Coleen confesses that she found it hard not to stick her nose into their business too much. 'When my granddaughter comes over for the day, it is difficult not to be a bit interfering,' she says. 'I've had to really bite my tongue and walk out because I do want to do it all.'

But Coleen hopes that her kids and their partners seek out any handy parental advice she can offer them, as she remembers when she was a first-time mum she needed all the help she could get. 'The funny thing is that I found after I had my baby it was the only time in my life when I desperately wanted to know what everyone else thought,' she says. 'I felt so lost, like, "What do I do with this? What do I do with that?" That's why I just loved having family around.'

However, while she was grateful for her mother-in-law's assistance, she did find her a little overbearing. 'I remember when I first had Shane Jr, I really relied on my mother-in-law because I lived in London and all my family lived up north. She used to come round and she was great. But she was very hands-on, interfering maybe, and would say, "When he's with me, he will live by my rules, not yours." So if I said to her, 'Oh, he does this then', she'd tell me, "Just go, because I'll get him into my routine."

When he got older there was a haircut that was trendy that I hated on boys. It was called the step and it just used to look like a bowl. I went on and on about this haircut, but when I came back off tour he had it! I actually do love her, I still love her she is great, but you know...!'

Saira says that while her mum isn't exactly an interfering busybody, she is a very naughty, sneaky grandma! 'I've told my mum not to give the children sweets and she agrees,' she laughs. 'Then when she leaves, I find all sorts of sweet wrappers under her pillow because she's been giving them midnight feasts!'

HAVE YOU TURNED INTO YOUR MOTHER?

As much as we love our mum, and as well intentioned as she may be, we usually don't really want to turn into her. And yet, as we start our own families, we often find ourselves making the same rules for our kids that we resented having to follow when we were growing up. And when you look in the mirror, do you ever see your mother staring back?

Saira is adamant that she and her mother could not be more different. 'I'm nothing like my mother,' she says. 'I love her to bits but she is very bossy, a bit of a control freak and really cynical and highly opinionated. Totally not like me at all. Haha! I'm joking. I am just like my mother. Only, I didn't realise we were so similar until the rest of the Loose Women pointed it out!'

Coleen says that when she was young, she made a pact with herself that one day when she had kids of her own, she would make sure she was nothing like her own mum. 'She used to say all these things and I'd tell myself that I would never say that to my children,' she says. 'However, now I say them myself and in the same way my mum used to say them! Not only that, I definitely take after my mum looks wise.'

LOOSE LESSONS

- Always talk with your parents about how much grandparent duty they are happy to do. You don't want to make them resent the relationship, so they should feel happy about it!

- If you need help and are struggling, always ask your parents or your parents-in-law to see if they can offer any words of wisdom.

- It's inevitable that you will one day say to your kids all those things your mum said to you, which you swore you'd never do. It will happen. And that is OK.

PART 6
BODY BATTLES

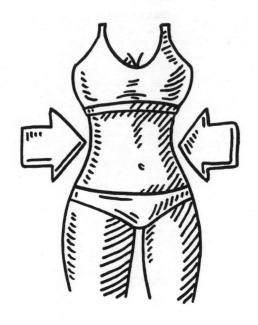

Try as we might, it's not easy for many of us to fall in love with our own bodies, even when people tell us how great we look. We look at ourselves in a mirror and a nasty voice in our heads points out all the bits that we simply hate. And no matter how much someone disagrees with us, if we think our nose is too big, then we still believe that it's the biggest ever seen. But why are we like this? Why do we look at ourselves and think the worst? Is it because we constantly compare ourselves to the images of perfection we see in magazines or on social media or on the TV? But we're cleverer than that, surely? We know that what we see in the media is the result of a lot of great lighting, an army of make-up artists and a little bit of Photoshop to ensure that the image is as glossy as can be. Ultimately, though, we all tend to grow up holding on to any negative comments that have struck home and find it incredibly hard to shrug them off. But finding our body confidence can be done. There is a way we can acknowledge the bits we like and learn to accept, as our Loose Women have proven.

BODY CONFIDENCE

HOW DO YOU FEEL ABOUT YOUR NAKED BODY?

Even when we're with someone really special who makes us feel great, it can be hard to completely let go of those pesky body insecurities. On the one hand, we're being told these days to be proud of who we are and celebrate our imperfections, while, on the other, media and advertising are constantly showing us images of the 'perfect' body type we should be aspiring to.

But there's been a change in perception, thanks in part to the Body Stories campaign that *Loose Women* launched in 2017. The campaign was inspired by a viewers' poll that revealed that 97 per cent of those who took part were unhappy with the way they looked and featured the cast of the show stripping down to their underwear for a photo shoot and embracing their realistic bodies. Viewers flocked to congratulate the women on their courage to be so open about their bodies.

The tide is turning, and recently adverts and magazines have started to show different body shapes and sizes, which is just so refreshing. The front cover of *Cosmopolitan* magazine that featured plus-sized model Tess Holliday 'kissing goodbye' to outdated beauty standards won an award; Boots' 2019 summer advertising campaign poked fun at the unobtainable 'beach body' and even swimwear–underwear retailers like Figleaves have begun using women with a range of body shapes to model their bikinis.

Of course, we all have parts of our bodies that we would like to improve. Even supposedly perfect people will cite something that makes them feel uncomfortable. So the next time we look in the mirror and see something we don't like, let's remember there is someone else out there experiencing the same woes.

Janet says she happily took part in the *Loose Women* Body Stories campaign because she wanted to help women her age feel they are part of this world. 'A lot of women my age feel invisible. They feel ashamed of what's under their clothes,' she says. 'The reason why I took my clothes off and posed in a swimsuit is because I think I look great. I never take my clothes off and think, "What an apology for a body". When I look at my body, I think it looks great, but I'm not thinking, "I'll walk round the block now and see what I can pick up." All the partners I've had have been complimentary and given me confidence, which I had anyway. Women my age should stop being ashamed of themselves. Everybody gets wrinkles.'

Nadia agrees that she felt empowered by taking part in the campaign but admits she is yet to come to terms with fully embracing her naked body. If anything, she is still reluctant to expose it, even at home in front of her husband.

'I felt so much better after doing the Body Stories shoot; I can go swimming now and not feel bad,' she laughs. 'But nudity, no way. Mark says I put on more clothes to go to bed than I do to go out.'

Oddly, Nadia comes from a family where nudity has never been a big issue. 'My mum is nude all the time,' she reveals. 'I came into the house a while back and was calling for her and found her stark naked, hoovering.'

Gloria admits that nudity wasn't part of her home life. 'Growing up in a two-up two-down in the forties and fifties, there wasn't much nakedness around,' she says. 'It was quite the opposite. And as a result I have always been quite modest.'

Saira was brought up in a culture in which, she explains, 'if you show any skin, you'll bring shame on the family'.

'I never saw my mum and dad naked,' she says. 'Mum was always covered from her neck to her feet all of her life.'

However, Saira says she is much more open with her kids and

isn't embarrassed for them to see her in the nude.

'I don't want them to be embarrassed about naked bodies,' she explains. 'So if my kids walk in I don't shy away. I want them to see that this is what a real body looks like. I want them to have a healthy attitude to the way we all look.'

She adds that appearing on *Loose Women* taught her to realise that she has a healthy and normal body and has been encouraged to embrace it. 'I'm not perfect,' she says. 'I think society has brainwashed us to believe we have to have this ideal figure that we can never have.'

Jane is another Loose Woman who is not the type to walk about in the nude. 'I don't walk around naked at home,' she says. 'Even when it's really hot, I never sleep naked. I worry there might be a fire and I'll have to run outside. But if I am naked and see myself I don't get bent out of shape about it. It is what is. It's the body I have got. I admire those women who can play naked volleyball but I couldn't do that. I'm happy to walk around my bathroom naked but not in public.'

Saira reckons we should look at ourselves more regularly in the mirror and rather than seeking out the bits we don't like, appreciate instead what we do have. 'We should be able to look at ourselves and say, "I'm all right."'

But it has taken her years to embrace her body. 'Because of my cultural background and because I was abused by my uncle at 13, I always had a lack of confidence in my body. I had never thought I was an attractive person, I was never told I was. I never thought men fancied me. Beauty for me has always been about how nice you are, but I am becoming more confident as I get older.'

Nadia wholeheartedly agrees. 'I'm an advocate for that,' she says. 'I look in the mirror and find the things I like, starting with the smallest thing. I have the best acceptance of my body that I have had all of my life.'

But Gloria admits that she's never been overly happy with her body although she has tried her best to keep in shape. 'It isn't always easy, as we know,' she reflects. 'But I would be classified as pre-diabetic, and so I had to lose weight. I had to give up sweet things, carbs and such like. Not that I have given it all up. But I lost two stone immediately – I couldn't stop it falling off. But it was actually too much and I wouldn't want to do that again. So I think you have to be very careful about how much weight you take off at any time, especially as you get older.'

IS SOCIAL MEDIA TO BLAME FOR POOR BODY POSITIVITY?

So we've made a resolution to stop looking in the mirror to identify all the faults we can find with our bodies, but when you're spooling through social-media platforms like Instagram and see the thousands of glossy pictures of immaculate and body-perfect people, do you start to feel down? How do they maintain their taut bodies, with zero blemishes and great skin tone? It's enough to make you want to hide. But let's pause for a moment. There are various points that you MUST remember if you're going to spend any time at all on social media. 1) That posted picture is probably the millionth shot they took, trying to get it exactly right. 2) It's been filtered and highlighted (there are lots of apps that essentially Photoshop all the 'bad' bits out. 3) If they are fit and scarily toned, well, that's because they are probably slaves to the gym, which we could be too if we really could be bothered.

But even though we know that what they are putting out there is an illusion, we can't help but feel a bit inadequate. So how do we stop ourselves from buying into these depictions on social media?

Nadia says she thinks things are beginning to change, that after a backlash against social media for being awash with unrealistic and doctored images, people are now taking a stand – including her daughter. 'I feel quite hopeful. I know there is a lot of negativity about social media, but there always have been a lot of images flashed at women, showing what we're "supposed" to be,' she explains. 'But Maddie will purposely post photos of herself when she isn't looking her best; she'll pull faces and post photos when she's got spots.'

However, Nadia is aware that some young kids are so affected by the artificial perfection seen online that many young boys and girls hardly dare leave their bedrooms. 'Maddie's got friends who won't go out – they're agoraphobic because they use filters so much that they then feel embarrassed to go out, because it's not really them,' she says. 'That's the negative side of that world, but I do think kids are starting to get fed up with it. Maddie said to me, "I know everything on social media isn't real because it's filtered, but when I go out with my friends I always think they look so much more beautiful."'

Coleen thinks that what Maddie says about her friends is something women of all ages can identify with. 'When I used to go out with my friends I always thought that they had what looked like the "perfect" figure,' she says. 'Even when we did the Body Stories campaign, I remember I told Nadia I felt vulnerable and that if I had her figure I'd walk around the supermarket naked! But everyone was still self-conscious.'

Saira says she doesn't believe social media is the main reason we are all so self-conscious about our bodies and who we are. 'It's all down to *me*. I do this to myself,' she declares. 'I open the fridge and go, "I won't have that, I'm having a fat day today" or "Doesn't my bum look big in this?" Actually, it's all this chitter-chatter between me and Steve at home that my kids pick up on. I said to Zac once, "Would you like some crisps?", and he said, "No, mummy, I think it's got too many calories in it. I'll have an apple." It's good to be healthy, but he's only 11!'

Nadia says she is very wary about the things she and Mark say at home in case she inadvertently encourages her kids to adopt habits or behaviour that might be damaging in the long run. 'That's the amazing thing: children teach us so much more than we teach them. They hold a mirror up to us and we see what we are doing to ourselves. That's the really hard thing, and I have to be conscious every day about what I say.'

Coleen laughs that her kids certainly haven't picked up any bad habits from her. In fact, they appear to be doing the exact opposite. 'My kids are really health-conscious,' she reveals. 'They are always going to the gym, always going running, but it's about health, because they want to feel better. They definitely haven't got that from me!'

HAS A LACK OF BODY CONFIDENCE HELD YOU BACK?

Insecurities can be a killer. How many times have we let a small aspect of our appearance – like a wrinkle – leave us feeling like Quasimodo on a bad day? Silly really, as we've all learned from experience that those little things that we worry about rarely get noticed by anyone around us. So when you tell your friend about how the appearance of a few grey hairs have ruined life as you know it, the odds are they will say, 'I hadn't even noticed.' And why? Because no one else fixates on a tiny facet of our appearance and blows it totally out of proportion – just us!

We are so worried about what others might think that we are unable to do things, fearful that someone will judge us. But there are a couple of ways of overcoming our issues. One, remember that everyone else is just like us. No matter how Hollywood pretty they are, they too are insecure about something, whether it's their hairline, wrinkles, chipped tooth or whatever. Second, we have to own our insecurity and quash it – to acknowledge that we have things we don't like but realise, in the grand scheme of things, that they are insignificant and not worth bothering about.

Kaye says that she has always been realistic about her looks and has learned not to be fixated by them. She says she will apply make-up when she needs to but otherwise she's just as happy without.

'If you were going to a wedding as a guest, you'd want to look your best. Whereas when I'm slobbing about at home, I look a total bag of spanners,' she laughs. 'I don't put on any make-up. Oh my God, I would frighten the children. And I'm more than happy to go out like that; it doesn't bother me at all. I knew at an early age that I was never going to get the boyfriend because of my looks. Because I couldn't compete. And you have to be realistic about that. Whoever handed out talents, it wasn't looks for me. I'm not saying that for an "Aw". What I'm saying is it's not just about looks. I've got other things.'

Nadia reminds her old pal that her woes about her looks never stopped her from anything. 'You're saying that, but you are a really confident person to your core.'

WHAT BODY-CONFIDENCE ADVICE WOULD YOU GIVE TO YOUR YOUNGER SELF?

Now we've reached a certain age and are more mature than ever, it's funny looking back on our younger selves and reminiscing about what worried us. When we were teenagers, we'd get upset over all sorts, mainly because we didn't have the life experience to understand how to turn things into strengths. In those days, we'd say we hated our curly hair only to think years down the line, 'Wow, that's my unique selling point.'

So what would we say to our younger selves to reassure them that a lot of things they are worried about are going to turn out just fine?

Nadia remembers her teen years as a rather negative time, when she mostly focused on what made her feel sad. But now, in her mid-fifties, she has made peace with the aspects of herself that caused her such pain. 'Back then, I used to say how much I hated things all the time,' she says. 'And now I'm over it. So I would say to myself, "Right now, right this minute, love your body. It will serve you so well, it will give you two wonderful children, and when you're 50, boy, will you miss it!"

Coleen agrees and says she would advise her teenage self not to worry about bumps and lumps and just love her body the way it is. 'I would say embrace your body shape now because it will go through many changes,' she says. 'And I'd also say focus more on what's on the inside because being a confident person is the most attractive thing in the world.'

Nadia reckons that our youthful obsession with fixating on the worst aspects of ourselves can be damaging as we navigate life. 'If you keep saying over and over again, "I hate my body, I hate my body" that will become your reality. I think you can turn the wheel and take a new pathway. As older and wiser men and women, we need to keep talking in a different way.'

All great advice, but it can be hard to listen and believe it at the time. 'I remember my mum telling me when I was young to stop focusing on my body and wait until I was her age,' says Coleen. 'The problem is, when you're younger, you don't listen to those who might know more. You have so many insecurities about everything that you don't listen. But you do get to an age where you go, "Actually, do you know what, I'm OK."'

DO WE WORRY THAT OUR PARTNER MISSES THE BODY THEY FELL IN LOVE WITH?

There's no getting away from it – whatever the big cosmetic companies try to tell us in their advertising campaigns. As we get older, wrinkles form and bodies sag. And for some of us, alongside anxieties about how we look as we age, we sometimes worry about what our partners might think of us. Are they happy with how we're maturing? Or are they secretly thinking about trading us in for a newer model?

Nadia seems to have nothing to worry about. Her husband knows exactly what to say! 'Mark's so good at that,' she says. 'I'll say to him, "Oh God, sorry about my cellulite, sorry about my boobs," and he will always look at me like I'm mad and say, "But you're asking me to separate a body part from who you are." He says, "I just can't do that. All of you, it's the whole thing."'

And Kaye thinks Mark isn't the only guy who is capable of appreciating us for who we are and not the body we used to have. 'Probably many more men would have that reaction than we think,' she muses. 'Some women sadly do get their other halves criticising their bodies, but I don't think we should allow the conversation. If your guy is going to start saying that sort of thing, the answer is: sod off.'

SHOULD RELIGION STOP YOU FROM SHOWING OFF YOUR BODY?

Everywhere you look, bodies are exposed. We see acres of flesh in magazines and music videos, on TV and at the cinema. When we see the stars of Love Island prancing about the villa in their barely there bikinis we hardly bat an eyelid, as we are so used to seeing men and women in varying states of undress. In a way, flesh-flashing has been become an acceptable way of life. Unless, of course, you have been brought up in a culture in which you are forbidden to show off any of your body at all.

When Saira took part in Loose Women's much lauded Body Stories campaign, she was devastated when she was inundated with cruel, critical messages from the Muslim community for daring to bare, even though the reasons behind it were important. 'I felt really sad that all my colleagues were getting so much praise, while I was getting criticism from some people from the Muslim community,' she says. 'One person wrote: "Your body parts are precious to you, as a Muslim I am disgraced to see this. You are a role model for many and this is not the way. If you wanted to do this to yourself you didn't need to make it public. May Allah forgive us; we are certainly living in difficult times but we need protection from the evil that's driving us to make what's wrong look right. Sorry if I said anything to hurt you, it was my duty to say it as a brother."'

Initially, Saira didn't react to the letter or to the other negative messages that she was sent following the campaign, but after a while she could no longer take the criticism directed at her and at her family. 'I kept my mouth shut for a very long time,' she explains. 'But I decided to confront this head on because I've had enough of people having a go at my mum for the things that I decide to do. I'm 47 years old, I'm married, I've got two children, and I eventually felt confident to say enough is enough.'

Saira explains that she signed up to Body Stories to say, 'Look, I am a Muslim, and I'm very happy to take part in this campaign. It has helped lots of women of colour to accept, "Yeah, our bodies look like that, we're a bit darker, we've got stretchmarks, a bit of a belly, we are normal too,"' she says. 'And what hurt me was people saying I was evil, that as a Muslim I'm representing evil. Me in a bikini is not evil. Me killing innocent people in the name of my religion, that would be evil. Let's get some perspective.'

Aware that the comments were from people who represented a small section of the Muslim community, she bravely fired back at the letter writer in no uncertain terms. 'My response was to call him a misogynistic, backward, brainwashed, idiotic person!' she says defiantly. 'That's what I thought. I wanted to do it to say, "Do you know what, for me as a woman – forget my religion, forget my colour – just as a woman to be able to feel confident and just stand there and say at long last, I'm really happy. I'm happy that I'm healthy, I'm happy that I was able to have a child, I'm happy that I'm not perfect, but I wanted to be part of this campaign with my colleagues and my work, and my religion doesn't stop me doing that.'

HOW WOULD YOU COPE IF YOU LOST YOUR HAIR?

Ask most women what their favourite feature is and many will more than likely say their hair. Yes, their crowning glory and all those clichés. But hair is really important to us. We spend loads on products, hours styling it; when we feel it looks great it tops off a great outfit and gives us confidence. But how would we feel if we suddenly started losing it? Would it make us feel less of a woman?

Nadia says she was devastated when she first discovered that her hair was thinning. It's hard to believe, as her gorgeous curls look so vibrant and springy. But she says her hair is now 'a quarter of what it used to be'.

'It started with a little patch at the front going, then more and more hair kept coming out,' she explains. 'My hair really started to change after I had my kids. Bloody kids! I not only lost a lot, like loads of mums do, but also the texture began to change. So from having really natural curly hair, my hair became frizzy. Then when I started to go into peri-menopause, I seemed to lose a third of my hair. People say to me all the time, "Oh my God, your hair's so thick, your hair's so amazing," but it's not.'

Concerned about losing her pride and joy, Nadia visited a specialist who told her she had the male-pattern balding gene. "'You either have the gene or you don't; you don't just lose hair because you're getting older," he told me. He said, "I can see all the follicles that have closed and out of which hair will never grow again." It was just devastating for me, as I do define myself by my hair.'

However, she also feels embarrassed about getting so upset about her hair loss, bearing in mind there are women who lose their hair for much more serious reasons. 'I feel really shallow talking about it. I feel bad even saying this when you think of people who have lost their hair completely with alopecia or from cancer treatment. But it doesn't really make it any easier, the fact that I'm losing my hair. I talked about it ages ago on *Loose Women*, and lots of people since have said to me, "God, I'm the same, it's the menopause".'

Luckily for Nadia she has a team of make-up artists and stylists at the *Loose Women* studios who can help tease her gorgeous hair into a full and bouncy masterpiece. 'I get so many tweets about my hair and I feel like such a fake,' she confesses. 'Our make-up people are amazing and they spend a lot of time on my hair. We hear about men feeling emasculated when they lose their hair, but I think it applies to women too – when we lose our hair, we feel defeminised.'

WOULD YOU HAVE A NIP AND TUCK?

These days, there are surgical procedures you can have done during a lunch hour. It sometimes seems like everyone's having some kind of nip and tuck at the moment, even when they don't really need it. But is it really necessary to go under the knife to make yourself look better or can we just be clever and enhance our looks in other, more simple and less invasive ways?

Even though she has never actually had any work done, Nadia fantasises about having a couple of bits improved. 'I would absolutely love to have my neck done because, after years of sunbathing and not listening to medical advice, I've now got a neck that doesn't portray how I feel about myself,' she explains. However, she says there is one big reason why she would never let herself get tweaked by a surgeon.

'I think that, if I didn't have children, I'd probably do it – but it would be such a bad example to set for my daughters.'

Not that her daughters would ever consider cosmetic surgery. Nadia says that because they haven't been around kids who worry about their looks, they have a very healthy attitude toward their bodies. 'My kids are very alternative and don't feel the same pressures as other children because they're home-schooled. They're very anti-surgery,' she says. 'One day I casually asked Kiki how she'd feel if I had a neck lift, and she said, "Tell me, right now, you are not having one!" I thought, "Damn, I can't ever have one!" They're not telling me what to do exactly, but they're coming at me from the point of view of what I've instilled in them – which is you have to be who you are – and now I have to practise what I preach and I'm really regretting it!'

Gloria admits that she is seriously thinking about having a spot of work done to eradicate some wrinkles on one side of her face. 'The more wrinkles that appear on my face, the more I do think, "Oh my God!"', she laughs. 'I haven't had any surgery yet, but I am considering having some because I just feel I don't want this to get any worse.

'When Caron died I couldn't even consider doing anything for vanity. Because I watched her for seven years fighting an illness, so I just couldn't bear to think, "Oh, I've got a few wrinkles here and there, I'll go and get a facelift." But I'm kind of over that bit now because sufficient time has passed.'

However, don't expect Gloria to end up looking like the Bride of Wildenstein. She would be very cautious as she has seen the damage that can be done by women who go too far. 'Carol McGiffin doesn't look like she's been stretched and I think Sharon Osborne's is amazing, but these young girls having surgery is just tragic,' she sighs. 'I look at them and they are beautiful as it is, but they are beginning to look all alike. Straight long hair, the trout pout, the self-tanning. And I just think, "You're all the same." I'm actually very bad at looking after myself beauty wise. I have only ever had two facials in my whole life. Now I think I am ready to get that nip and tuck, but I need to pluck up the courage to do it.'

Saira says she would never go under the knife. 'I am 50 next year and I have noticed my skin is getting a bit saggy but I will never have surgery,' she admits. 'That said, I don't mind a bit of Botox or a non-invasive procedure that will give me a lift. I am vain and I want to look the best I can, but I don't want people to say, "You look like a goldfish." I don't want to look 20 when I am 80.'

She also says that she is horrified by women as young as 18 who are undergoing work to improve their looks. She believes they are making big mistakes and are lacking good parents.

'These teenagers who are having Botox and surgery have low self-esteem and a lack of love in their lives. I have to ask, where are the parents? The thing is these girls don't realise that men don't even like the look. I know a lot of young men who say that they'd get together with these girls on a night out but wouldn't take them home to meet mum. The more natural you are, the more self-esteem you will have, and that makes you more attractive.'

Saira believes that girls should be more themselves if they want to succeed. 'I find it difficult when I see girls who are obsessed with their looks,' she says. 'I have a degree and got through life without lots of make up. I have done a lot of sport so I see my body as a machine, not a sexual object. It's strong and it does what I want it to do. I don't have big boobs or long legs. I don't judge myself against supermodels. I have never spent too much time worrying about it. And that gives you body confidence.'

LOOSE LESSONS

- Start the message very young and encourage your kids to love their bodies.

- Don't put yourself down in front of the kids as it could leave a lasting impression on them.

- Love your own body. Embrace the body you have been given as it will go through so many changes over your lifetime.

DIETING AND FITNESS

IS EVERYDAY WEIGHING A GOOD IDEA?

 There used to be a time when every TV show or magazine would be offering us a million ways to lose weight. Come New Year, everywhere you looked, there'd be a streamlined celeb flashing their six pack and boasting about how they shed the pounds in a record amount of time. Even if we were happy with our bodies at the time, the constant visibility of skinny celebs talking about their 'easy' way to shed pounds and we'd be convinced to try it too.

And with that pressure comes constant scrutiny. How much looser does that dress feel? How much belly fat can we squeeze? How many pounds have we lost? When we are on these diets we become so obsessed with how well we are doing that we check our progress constantly and feel disappointed if we're not seeing results fast enough.

But can it be healthy to get on the scales regularly, to ensure that we keep our weight in check? According to some experts, daily weight checks could help us lose weight because if we can see we are losing weight it will encourage us to build healthier habits...

'I haven't got any scales. I don't see the point,' Janet says. 'Basically, you go to the cupboard and get out something you want to wear, and if it's a bit tight, don't have a bacon sandwich in the morning! But I've noticed my partner's got scales and I say, "Throw them out!" because I think men are more obsessed with weighing themselves now. Once the waistband starts to expand, they think, "I just won't have lunch or I won't eat today," and somehow the weight will drop off. They don't have a plan.'

Janet also says that those exercise junkies who are pumping iron at the gym should remember that when they do workouts involving weights, they are more likely to gain weight than lose it. 'Muscle weighs more than flab,' she points out. 'So the whole business about weight and weighing yourself is a tyranny.'

Saira says she is confused about how to lose weight these days as all the methods that were once preached about have turned out to be a load of baloney! 'The science about how you lose weight has radically changed. When we were growing up, it was all about low-fat yoghurts and how you had to do 100 crunches to get a flat stomach, but that is now all rubbish!' she says. 'Now the science says that low-fat stuff was laden with sugar, so it was counter-intuitive. I do think what Janet says say about clothes is right. Just go by the size of your clothes. That said, clothes sizes are different in each store – in one particular shop I might be a size 8, in another I might only fit into a size 12.'

DO CELEBRITY-FITNESS DVDS HELP US LOSE WEIGHT?

For years we snapped up celebrity-fitness DVDs to help us ditch the weight and we loved them. For one, we didn't have to go to a gym and humiliate ourselves in front of a roomful of strangers and figure out how to use all the intimidating equipment. Instead, we could happily work up a sweat with our favourite stars in our own living room, dressed in whatever we wanted.

So popular were these DVDs that the industry made hundreds of thousands of pounds from people unhappy with their bodies and looking for an easy fix. And we have snapped them up over the years in the desperate hope that they can help us transform our bodies into the one we desire most.

And our Loose Women think that these DVDs can be helpful because they give us something easy to follow and inexpensive to use in order to get a bit fitter.

'For me, I have no issue with fitness DVDs. If you're in your living room and you're moving around a bit more, great,' Jane says. 'But the weight-loss ones are selling a myth to people. As a journalist, I see a reality star pictured on a beach supposedly unaware and looking overweight and then the next thing that you know they have a weight-loss DVD coming out. Come on, we know it's a set-up!'

One celeb who has fronted her own fitness DVDs is Coleen. Unlike many fitness-DVD stars, she even managed to keep the weight off and stay fit for almost four years!

'I've done three actually. And they came at a really good time for me too, because I was getting to that age and I'd not long had Ciara, and I was overweight,' she recalls. 'But it was hard, you had to really put the effort in. I was training six, seven days a week. I didn't have food sent to me; it was more about the fitness. But obviously there's no point in being fit and dancing for an hour if you're then going to sit down and eat twelve slices of pizza, so it was about food as well. But I have to say, all mine really worked and I kept the weight off for three and a half years. But then life becomes involved and you haven't got the trainer every day.'

Coleen remembers that when she was busy working out for her hit DVD regime, she'd end up comparing herself to other celebs who were doing their own rival DVDs. 'I would look at other people doing theirs and think, "They look like they've lost a stone since last week! What are they doing that I'm not?"' she recalls. 'But now looking back and hearing those stories I realise that it's because I was doing it the right way, losing two to three pounds a week. Initially quite a lot comes off. They did work, but it's the keeping going that's the hard and important bit.'

DO SLIMMING CLUBS WORK?

You've tried doing a diet on your own, but it didn't work. You signed up to the gym but quit after a week of hiding in the changing rooms. You stocked up on all the celeb-fitness DVDs but stuck them in a cupboard after a couple of weeks. So, what now...? How are you going to shift that excess weight? Slimming clubs are more popular than ever. Some people find that the diet plan and weekly weigh-ins have encouraged them to shed the pounds like magic. So are slimming clubs worth the effort? Are they a better way for us to shed? And just how cringey are those weekly weigh-ins?

One Loose Woman who swears by slimming clubs is Coleen, who says she has a lot to thank them for. 'I've joined them all, and whatever you put in your mouth, you think, "Oh God, I'm going to be weighed on Friday," she says. 'What was great for me and my mates was on a Friday it was like a night out for us, because we would go along, get weighed, pat each other on the back for losing a pound and a half, get a badge and then, feeling proud of ourselves, we'd go off and have a Chinese! Because you'd have a week then to get it off!'

While Coleen is an advocate of diet clubs, Janet isn't entirely convinced. 'I don't believe in diets. I don't think they work,' she says. 'Slimming clubs are probably a good way of making friends. But not a good way of losing weight, let's be honest.'

But Coleen is adamant that it is sensible eating that leads to weight loss and slimming is doable, with a few provisos. 'They do work, but the problem is that you have to be in the right mindset to work hard, which is where I struggle,' she confesses. 'And the thing is, once you reach your target weight, you think, "I don't need to go back now because I'm the weight I want to be." Then you return to your old habits. And it's the kind of thing that when you've learned how to do it, you really have to stay in the mindset of, "I need to do this now, forever. There is no end."'

Janet thinks that faddy diets are just a myth and believes in a straightforward eating plan and perhaps even counselling. 'Isn't it better to get up in the morning and be happy with yourself the way you are, eat a little bit of what you like and just feel well-balanced and happy and have friends anyway?' she says. 'I think people looking to lose weight need counselling, not Weight Watchers. But I don't want to denigrate all slimming clubs because I think they fulfil a valuable function, which is people make friends there, and there's a kind of community.'

When Gloria married her second husband Stephen twenty years ago they both went on a diet. 'We lost around a stone in weight, I lost a stone and Stephen lost ten pounds, and my wedding dress looked great on me as a result!'

WILL EATING FROM SMALLER PLATES MAKE US THIN?

When experts suggested that the secret to weight loss was to eat from smaller plates, we thought, 'D'oh!' Unless you pack that tiny plate of yours with sugary treats like doughnuts, Haribo and Snickers, of course, having less on a plate should encourage some kind of weight loss as there is – surprise, surprise – fewer calories sitting on it.

Coleen can see the benefits of this sensible idea but says having come from an Irish family of big eaters it's not an easy concept to get used to. 'I think they're right in the respect of it's not necessarily what you're eating, it is the quantity, and that's what every specialist would tell you,' she says. 'I definitely need smaller portions. But I grew up in an Irish household and if your mother was like my mother, she piled it on, and you weren't allowed to leave the table until your plate was clear.'

But if she thought her mum's servings were generous, a trip to America left her slack jawed. 'Honestly it's quite horrifying the portion sizes over there,' she says, still rather dumbstruck. 'I took the kids to a well-known fast-food restaurant, and I said just get regular, because they always get large meals here, and their regular drink was bigger than our large drink over here. Honestly, it was like a bucket. And one day I ordered an omelette and it was the biggest omelette I'd ever seen. I said to the woman, "That omelette's so big!" She said, "Yeah, we put 18 eggs in it!" I don't eat 18 eggs in a year, let alone in one breakfast sitting!'

Janet says she is fascinated by the fact that, since the beginning of the twentieth century, the size of dinner plates has increased considerably. 'I love that there's a word for it now, it's called overserving. It's true, they reckon plates have expanded 25 per cent; they've gone up a quarter in size since 1900,' she informs us. 'But the odd time I've eaten off small plates, it has worked. Once or twice I've gone to a spa and they serve up that ghastly mini-meal, which is three slices of grapefruit on a tiny plate. Then you have your lunch, which is a tiny bowl of soup, which you have to learn how to eat. And you do lose about five pounds in a week.'

But it's not just plates that have become much larger, Janet says, as so have glasses! 'Do you remember 20 years ago when a wine glass was quite small?' she asks. 'Now if you go and buy them at IKEA or any of these chainstores, a normal wine glass is like a bucket on a stalk! But my top tip for drinking less is to find – at a jumble sale or the back of your mum's cupboard – those old sherry glasses. Now, if I think I'll have a little predrink drink in the early evening it's a sherry glass of wine.'

ARE YOU AN OVEREATER?

We hear a lot about eating disorders, mainly anorexia and bulimia. But less talked about is binge eating, when people gobble down as much as they can in a sitting, normally to temper their frantic emotions when they are in a dark place. Nadia bravely opened up on the show about her struggle with binge eating, explaining that for her it was a habit that started out in childhood. 'I didn't know it when I was growing up but I know now that I was a compulsive eater and that I used to binge eat to suppress my emotions.'

From the outside, Nadia says people might not have thought she had any problems in life, but as time went on and her self-esteem hit rock bottom, she turned to food to solve her overactive imagination. 'I was a very happy person and had a very happy childhood. I loved my life,' she recalls. 'But I also had a long period of my life when my eating was out of control. And not in the way that somebody just overeats and can be a bit greedy. I ate to shut out things that I didn't want to feel and because I had such low self-esteem.'

She says that although her mum and dad had a very healthy attitude towards food, a lot of people in her extended family were very overweight and would say things to her like, 'If you love me, will you eat this?' as well as saying, 'Have you put on a little weight?'

Nadia explains that her low self-esteem was so extreme that it caused her a lot of heartache. 'I used to cry about how fat I thought I was,' she recalls. 'And I always used to do this thing where I would overeat. While somebody feeling a bit down might have a couple of pieces of toast, I would have the whole loaf. And I remember instances when I would be in a restaurant and I'd be sitting opposite somebody just talking to them, and then I'd realise the bread basket we had between us had been emptied. The terrible thing was I wouldn't even remember eating it. But I'd panic and look at the other person and realise there was no bread. So, if they hadn't eaten it, then it could have only been me.'

These days, Nadia has a much healthier relationship with food. 'I am very, very different about my food now than when I was young,' she explains. 'Food is there to nourish me, to nourish my family. I love to cook, I love to eat, but I no longer eat to shut out my feelings. And I know there'll be so many people reading this today who might just have finished off a whole packet of biscuits without even realising it.'

ARE WE ALL GUILTY OF JUDGING PEOPLE ON THEIR APPEARANCE?

Whether we realise it or not, we all judge people on first impressions. Even before they open their mouths, we make an instant decision about someone based on what they look like. Think about it: when a new person starts in your office, do you not immediately try to work out what kind of personality they have based on the length of their skirt, style of their hair and the amount of make-up they are wearing? It's unfair, but we do it.

Individuality and being confident enough to wear whatever we like is one thing, but Saira still believes that we should always make sure we present ourselves in a way that is appropriate to the situation. 'Imagine I was wearing a low-cut leopard-print top and denim hot pants, big hoops and heels. What impression am I giving off? Well, I wouldn't wear that to a business interview or to pick the kids up from school. I do think you have to wear appropriate clothes for appropriate situations. And that is just the way that I've been brought up. But it also worked for me. I've been in business; I've been in corporate boardrooms. If I was dressed in hot pants and a crop top I'd be laughed out of the room.'

However, some people judge others not just on what they wear but on their size too, which Janet thinks is incredibly unfair. 'To judge people on their body type and make remarks about someone's figure is absolutely disgusting and inappropriate. But the fact is, unconsciously, most of us choose to dress appropriately. We make all sorts of decisions. So when you go to work you wear one set of clothes; when you go out with your mates, you wear another.'

Janet argues that if someone with an IQ of 167 were to wear the outfit Saira suggested to a job interview for a hotel receptionist, for example, she would most likely not be taken seriously. 'The outfit doesn't make you any less of a woman or less intelligent or anything else,' she says. 'But in that workplace scenario, people are coming into a hotel, where they might be paying hundreds of pounds a night for a room, and they want to be met by someone who takes their job seriously. And whether you like it or not, that is not an outfit that a hotel receptionist would wear! Behind a bar maybe.'

While there has been much criticism of the likes of Little Mix and Rihanna for adopting highly sexualised images, which are digested mainly by impressionable youngsters, Janet maintains that there are worse personas to be associated with. 'For me, there's something else that's just as bad as kids seeing images of women with very little on, and that's the Disneyfication of women,' she says. 'The virginal look. That image of womanhood for me is just as nauseating.'

Saira says, 'I think the way you choose to dress expresses who you are. And if I were wearing the hot pants and crop top combo, I think I'd feel highly sexualised. And the only person who would like me to open the door like that every night would be my husband!'

LOOSE LESSONS

- It is all well and good thinking a celeb-fitness DVD will change your life, but the most important things are eating well and regular exercise. Do think about joining a slimming club for support.

- If you are trying to keep your weight down, one of the best things to do is to eat smaller portions. You can enjoy what you eat, but in moderation.

- Unfortunately, we do sometimes make judgements about people, but strive not to judge them on their body type and definitely don't make any casual remarks about someone's figure – you don't know how they feel about themselves and their relationship with their body.

PART 7
STAYIN' ALIVE

When we're young, we think we're invincible. We believe that nothing in the world can stop us and that we'll live for ever. But as we know, life is complicated, and there are many twists and turns to contend with on our path through it.

These days some of us have got into the habit of talking more about things that bother us. If you are worried about something – like having a smear test or even if there's just an unresolved issue bouncing around in your head – don't keep quiet, tell someone. Of course you might need to chat to someone more experienced to help overcome your problems, but just sharing your worries is hopefully the first step to making you feel like you are no longer alone.

COPING WITH THE MOST DIFFICULT TIMES

OPENING UP ABOUT MENTAL HEALTH

 Once upon a time, more often than not, mental-health issues were swept under the carpet. Whenever we felt blue, we kept the troublesome feelings to ourselves and tried to carry on with life regardless, while no one around us acknowledged they existed. Little did we know then that by stifling these feelings, the worse they could get, resulting sometimes in bursting out of us in ways we didn't expect. Luckily, shows like *Loose Women* have changed the landscape and normalised discussions about mental health and, as a result, have encouraged more and more people to start recognising their situations and find ways of making themselves feel better.

It will, of course, come as no surprise that with their decades of life experience, our Loose Ladies have all had their fair share of experiences of living with mental-health issues.

Coleen says that when her first marriage broke down after her husband's multiple infidelities she was devastated and was left in limbo, struggling to work out what to do next. 'I went through weeks of thinking "I can do this", and I wouldn't cry in front of anyone, and I certainly wouldn't cry in front of the kids,' she says of that sad time.

'I'd drop the boys off at school then go home and get straight back in to bed and then get up when it was time to pick them up again. That went on for two or three weeks. But then I thought, "Enough is enough, I need help, I can't do this on my own."'

Recognising that she couldn't carry on this way alone, Coleen decided she needed to seek professional advice, even though she felt a little embarrassed about doing so. 'I went to my NHS doctor and he put me in touch with a counsellor and I had counselling over six months,' she remembers. 'The first time I walked in, I was so embarrassed, I remember saying to my friends, "What am I going to say to this stranger? She doesn't even know me." I spent the first 25 minutes sobbing and I'd never cried before in front of anyone like I did then. It was brilliant having somebody there who had no preconceptions of me; not a family member. And all she did over a period of time was put logic back into my way of thinking because everything was just out of control.'

The sessions were a revelation to her because she had never really believed in counselling up until that point. 'I'd be like, "You don't need it, you can sort it out,"' she says. 'It worked so amazingly for me and at the end of the six months the counsellor said, "You don't need me any more." She had given me the strength I needed to move forward.'

Janet understands the ways mental-health issues can grip a mind and cause a person to struggle. 'What happens is, you don't realise it's happening to you, that you're slipping out of seeing things normally,' she reflects. 'I think it's a gradual process where small things assume gigantic proportions; you get everything out of kilter and you don't realise it's happening. It's quite a subtle thing so it doesn't necessarily need to be triggered by splitting up with someone or a death in the family, it might just be happening to you in a small way.'

Janet says when she was younger her mother was dealing with mental-health issues that were not treated. 'When she got older, I saw my mother retreat,' Janet says. 'She stopped answering the phone, she stopped seeing people, she stopped eating. It was really hard to reach out to her, and I was probably the wrong person to help her as I was her daughter.'

Janet has found herself falling into a dark place at various points and was only pulled out when a friend intervened. 'A few years back, I got into a bad state and a really close friend wrote me a letter that said, "You're becoming a total pain in the arse; you've got to get a grip." I can laugh about it now and it is quite comical, but it wasn't comical for the people around me, it wasn't comical at all.'

Janet says that people look at her and think of her as confident, that she is someone who can cope with everything thrown at her, but she says that is a façade. She advises that if you feel low about something visit your GP or call the Samaritans. 'I want people to know that they can pick up a phone and speak to someone and that's step one,' she says. 'It shouldn't be someone, you know because the only way you can talk from the bottom of your heart is to an anonymous person.'

SHOULD WE FEEL GUILTY ABOUT ABORTION?

Anyone who has brought up a child knows how all consuming it can be. So it stands to reason that not all women feel ready or able to become a mum. Perhaps they feel too young to take on the role or maybe they just don't feel emotionally or financially equipped to care for a little one at the time. Possibly something terrible has happened and carrying a baby to birth isn't an option for that woman.

In the UK, women have had the option to legally terminate a pregnancy since 1967 when the Abortion Act was passed. At the time of writing, however, it remains illegal in Northern Ireland, which means women there seeking a termination have to travel to the mainland for the procedure.

In 2019, Janet expressed her disgust that various states in the US had passed a bill that made it illegal for women to undergo an abortion after six weeks unless the mother's life was in danger – or at all in the case of Alabama. She said she found it 'very, very chilling that in the 21st century women are still not in charge of their own bodies'.

The subject of abortion is very close to home for Janet as she had two terminations in her teens at a time when the procedures were illegal.

'When I was 16 or 17 I was doing my exams and I found out I was pregnant,' she recalls. 'I just didn't know what to do and back then abortions were illegal – they were very, very hard to get.'

Because she didn't have a particularly close relationship with her parents, she had to seek help from the friends that she had made out on the club scene. 'I remember going up to the West End and asking around in clubs for pills that might end my pregnancy and taking a whole cocktail of dodgy drugs, but nothing happened, except I was really, really sick.'

Luckily someone came forward and gave her the help she needed, suggesting she should go to a backstreet abortionist in north London, where the procedure would set her back £25.

'I remember the walk from the station,' she says sombrely. 'I still dream about that walk. I walked along the road, went to the house, knocked on the door and went into a flat upstairs.'

There, a woman told her to get on the kitchen table where she carried out the procedure. Afterwards, Janet recalls how she walked back to the Underground and went home, and spent the next 24 hours blaming herself for falling pregnant.

'I thought, "How stupid was I?", because you blame yourself. But back then, contraception wasn't easy to get as it is now,' she says. 'Since that day, I have tirelessly campaigned that women have to be in charge of their own bodies and have access to terminations. I just find that in the 21st century, how can it be that in Northern Ireland the only way you can get an abortion is if there's a serious risk of loss of life? That's just not right.'

Janet isn't the only member of the *Loose Women* panel to have undergone the procedure. When Coleen was 16, she became pregnant by her boyfriend at the time, Robin Smith, a keyboardist for The Nolans. She knew that it was not the right moment in her life to start a family.

'Intuitively I knew I was pregnant,' she said. 'I woke one morning to a strange feeling of nausea, and in the back of my mind was the niggling reminder that I had lost my virginity four weeks earlier and we hadn't used anything.'

Both Coleen and Robin knew they were too young and not emotionally equipped to become parents and agreed it was best to end the pregnancy early on.

'I was six weeks pregnant and decided I couldn't have it,' she remembers. 'I was 16 and had just joined my sisters. My parents were Irish Catholics so I had never had a conversation about sex or boyfriends or anything. My parents passed away without ever knowing. Would my family have understood? I like to think so now, and I'm sure my sisters would have, but my parents...well, I just don't know.'

Although Coleen believes every woman should have the choice to have an abortion if she wants one, she does think the time limit of 24 weeks in the UK should be reduced by four weeks. 'It should be reduced to 20 weeks as 70 per cent of babies are surviving at 23 weeks. If you find out you are pregnant early on, you can make that decision earlier, so why wait so long?'

Kaye is in full support of women undergoing an abortion and feels that we need to change the vocabulary surrounding the procedure. Instead of saying that women 'live with guilt' after having an abortion, we should recognise that in most cases women go through with a termination knowing that it will make their lives better.

'This is what we have to stop,' she demands. 'Some women will feel guilty and that's their entitlement. But some women don't. When we talk about abortion, the second question is "Do you feel guilty?" It's always in the same sentence. Shame, guilt, abortion. Why do we make that assumption? I have friends who have had abortions, and it's been a difficult decision for them.'

CAN YOU EVER GET OVER A TRAUMATIC CHILDHOOD EXPERIENCE?

Back in November 2016, Saira shocked viewers when she opened up for the first time about a traumatic experience that had taken place when she was a child. While speaking about the campaigner

Mukhtar Mai – the teenage girl who had been gang-raped in Pakistan after her 12-year-old brother had been falsely accused of having an inappropriate relationship with someone – Saira revealed that a male family member once abused her in her bedroom when she was just 13.

'I would never have talked about it, but I just felt I had to because of what Mukhtar is trying to do and what she had said: "I just want to be a voice of these women who face circumstances similar to what I did." And her words inspired me to talk about something that happened to me that is wrong. And if any young child or woman is going through something – if somebody is touching them without their permission, inappropriately – please, it is wrong. Go and get some help. It is wrong, it is not culturally acceptable, it is not religiously acceptable, it is wrong. It happens every day in our homes as well as in villages in Pakistan. And I wasn't expecting to say that.'

Saira explained that the assault took place when she was 13 years old and was carried out by a family member who has subsequently died. She never told a soul before finally opening up to her mum and brothers, and then on the show.

'I talked to my mum about it years later, and she was amazing,' she remembers. 'I talk about it now because this man is dead and I feel like I got one over on him, but reading Mukhtar's story inspired me to not keep it a private thing.'

She says that when something like this is done to a child at a young age, they can rarely process what has happened to them until later, and it's only then that they realise the full gravity of what has happened.

She said at the time: 'As a child or a young person, you don't know how the abuse you've experienced is affecting you,' she explains. 'I think how it affected me was, from that moment, that incident robbed me of my childhood and of my innocence. And if it hadn't happened, I might be a different person. But now, as a 46-year-old woman, I look back at my life and what I've been like. I realise I was very angry, and I would ask myself, "Why did this happen to me; why do people do this to other people?" Especially somebody whom you're supposed to trust, who safeguards you.

'And so without even knowing it, my behaviour became aggressive and I was angry. And as soon as I was with people, there was a barrier. My experience led to a disconnect between my sexuality and my body – I found it very hard to love my body. I battled against my curves when I was younger as I didn't want boys to notice me for being sexy – I was brought up to never bare my skin in front of men – it took me a long time not to feel guilty for wearing a dress or baring my arms.'

Saira says she finally found a release and freedom from the past after she was able to come to terms with what had happened to her. As a result, everything about her that hadn't been sitting well, finally made complete sense for the very first time.

'When you come to a place where you can reflect on life and you're with other women who haven't experienced that, you wonder, "Why am I different?"' she says. 'And you start thinking and going back through events.'

After opening up about her ordeal, Saira decided to have counselling to deal with the delayed trauma of her experience, which she says was totally out of character for her. 'I'm the last person to ever admit that I needed counselling, because for me, in my mind and my generation, counselling is seen as a failure, a weakness,' she says. 'But I'm wrong, because I absolutely needed it. That ordeal robbed me of my innocence, and it robbed me of the person I could have been: a gentler person towards people and just generally.'

LIFE AFTER MISCARRIAGE

Finding out you are pregnant can be one of the most joyous, life-changing and exciting (but also slightly terrifying!) moments of any woman's life. While the result of the pregnancy is eagerly anticipated, mums-to-be can be filled with nerves and the worry about what is yet to come. Not only that, the pregnancy period is certainly not easy.

While it is often said that mums-to-be are positively glowing, let's not forget there is morning sickness, vomiting, aches and pains and a whole host of other unpleasant ailments that make the experience less joyful. However, pregnancy marks the start of a whole new chapter in your journey.

Sadly, however, not all pregnancies will last the full term. Miscarriage – the loss of the baby in the first 23 weeks of pregnancy – is relatively common. It is thought that around one in eight women who know they are pregnant will suffer a miscarriage. There are lots of reasons why this may happen, and while almost all are beyond anyone's control, it can be a devastating experience for the woman who loses her baby and her partner.

While we know miscarriage is something that has happened to many women, it's still not a topic that is often spoken about openly. There are a variety of reasons for this. Some prefer to deal with it in private, and find it painful to discuss, while others are afraid to open up to those around them in case they make others feel uncomfortable.

Nadia is lucky to have two healthy daughters, but for a while she thought she and Mark would never have children. She endured three miscarriages and found each of them hard to deal with.

Prior to the birth of their first daughter, Maddie, the couple suffered their first miscarriage, which Nadia and Mark dealt with privately, as no one else had been aware that she was even pregnant. At the time, she was needlessly frightened that this was a signal that she might not be able to have kids. She explains that the experience made her feel guilty about things she had done in her past – particularly an earlier abortion, even though doctors say that this procedure is very unlikely to affect a woman's future ability to conceive and carry a child.

'I had had a termination years before. And all that guilt came up,' she says. 'I was thinking, "Is this a punishment?" I immediately felt panic-stricken. What if I'm barren now and I can't have a baby?'

So when she became pregnant again and gave birth to a healthy Maddie, Nadia was very much relieved. However, after Maddie's birth, she suffered two more miscarriages. The third one was particularly devastating and traumatic: 'I actually had it at home and delivered it,' she recalls. 'I was about four and a half months pregnant; I actually kept the foetus in the freezer because I didn't want it to go anywhere. Because there's that connection, that lioness comes out. I wasn't able to do anything; I wasn't able to protect. I'm not ready to let go. Eventually, we had a burial for it and that was really good.'

Luckily, shortly after this horrific experience, she discovered she was pregnant once again. Although nervous that she might miscarry, she eventually gave birth to daughter Kiki-Bee. 'I was devastated after my miscarriages but as soon as I had Kiki I really did feel healed, because I felt it was always Kiki's soul trying to get through,' she says. 'With the previous pregnancies, there was the body and I lost the body, but a soul only came to me in Kiki.'

LOSING A LOVED ONE

Loose Women has campaigned regularly for its viewers to examine their breasts to check for any lumps or sudden changes. Early diagnosis often means a full recovery. Sadly, some women lose their battle with cancer, as many of the Loose Women have experienced in some ways. Coleen lost her sister Bernie to the disease and Gloria lost her daughter Caron Keating in 2004 after her long battle with breast cancer. Even now, Gloria finds it hard to talk about the loss of her daughter but is keen for women to remain vigilant when it comes to examining their breasts.

'I remember when Caron was first diagnosed I was in shock because she was only in her early thirties,' she recalls. 'At first, her doctor thought it was just a milk lump having had a baby a few months prior. And so she had that laissez-faire thing of, "It's just a lump, I shouldn't be here and shouldn't have this test." But then it was confirmed that it was cancer – that was one of the worst days of my life.'

Caron took the diagnosis calmly and entered into treatment with a positive attitude. However, Gloria was devastated and didn't take her daughter's diagnosis well. 'I remember waking up in the middle of the night once, some months into her diagnosis thinking to myself, "If I don't tap into her positivity, I could be under the bus long before anything happens to her."'

Gloria says that whenever she was around Caron, she was upbeat and made sure she was always there for her. But she praises Caron's husband Russ, as he was always on hand-making sure she had everything she needed. 'We called him "Saint Russ" because he was sensational.'

When the doctor broke the news to Caron after her mastectomy and radiotherapy that there was nothing more that could be done, he told her to go and live her life. 'Caron said, "I don't know what to do now,"' Gloria remembers. 'You've had your treatment and you think, "How do I go forward?" So Caron went forward with that positivity and we all tried to help her in this. And I think that's really important. She thought that all the feelgood factors like cleansing her blood, boosting her immune system, all gave her a purpose to lead her life as best she could to beat the cancer.'

Embracing that positive outlook, Caron and Russ went to live in Cornwall for a while and Australia too, which Gloria found hard to cope with initially. 'Of course, as a mother you don't want your daughter any further than around the corner, never mind dealing with cancer. So when she went to Australia, I couldn't quite understand why she had to go that far away. But I realised this is how she wanted to live her life – Australian sunshine, magnificent beaches and freedom.'

After Caron died in the UK in 2004, Gloria was devastated by her loss. She would later set up the Caron Keating Foundation, a fund-raising partnership set up to raise money to offer financial support to professional carers, complementary healing practitioners and support groups dealing with cancer patients, as well as individuals and families who are affected by the disease.

After Gloria had time to grieve, she saw life in a different way and actively sought out women who had been through the same loss as her.

'What her death has given me is a strong empathy for other people,' she says. 'Losing a child changes you; you can't be the same person. Through our foundation, mothers get in touch and I will actually ring those people if I can, because I remember feeling desperate to speak to another mother who had gone through the same thing.'

Even though fathers are also just as devastated by the death of a child, Gloria truly believes that the grief a mother feels is more intense. 'I'm not undermining a father's experience – but there's something about carrying and giving birth to that baby that gives you an extra depth of despair,' she explains.

Gloria admits that she did suffer severe depression, but she says she forced herself out of this. 'I had to pull myself together. I had two lovely sons, Paul and Michael, a lovely husband and grandchildren, and I told myself, "You have to stop this and go back to some form of normality."'

For a long while after Caron's death, Gloria thought she'd never find happiness again. But when *Strictly Come Dancing* came calling, her sons convinced her that this could be exactly what she needed to reboot her life. 'I actually never thought I'd laugh or smile ever again,' she remembers. 'I was in such a black hole and Michael said to me, "I find that so sad." But then when the call came in from *Strictly* I couldn't find anyone to tell me not to do it so I signed up.' And what a difference appearing on the show made to her life. 'This is where the joy came in; it allowed me an excuse to laugh and have joy. Anything that takes your mind off grief helps, I say. I'll never forget the warmth and positivity; to be able to do something that was just for me and allowed me to smile again for a bit.'

Gloria believes that in some ways Caron is still around. Every time she sees a single white feather, she believes that's her daughter's calling card. 'Caron introduced me to the whole philosophy of angels because she did some programmes and documentaries about them, and she totally believed that if she found an isolated white feather it was a sign of an angel,' she says. 'Now when I find that white feather, I like to believe that I am closer to Caron.'

Coleen's sisters Anne, Linda and Bernie have fought cancer, though sadly Bernie lost her battle back in 2013, which Coleen says was like a wake-up call for her. 'Her death changed me and my thought process about life,' she says. 'When someone so close to you dies, you do think of your own mortality. It made me think, "Oh God, am I happy?" I knew I needed to change things. Bernie didn't have that choice.'

Coleen says that even though the family don't have the BRCA gene, the fact three of her siblings have had cancer has encouraged her to keep an eye on changes in her body. 'The odds are against me with three sisters being diagnosed with cancer,' she says. 'That's why I'm very vigilant. I try not to get too paranoid about it because I don't want the fear to take over my life, but I want to catch it as early as possible, so it gives me a much bigger chance of surviving. Yes, I could get cancer, but I'm just going to try to enjoy life as much as possible and not get hung up on relationships or a marriage not working. I'm still alive. Life really is too short.'

Gloria concludes that there are amazing developments in the treatment for cancer. 'Everything has improved so much since Caron died,' she smiles. 'Machinery is improving all the time; the drugs are improving. It's still a swine of a disease but fewer people are dying from it.'

Saira too understands loss, after her father died of a heart attack when she was 28. 'Losing my dad was terrible; it was the first time I grieved. He had gone back to Kashmir for a long holiday with my mum, for the first time in thirty years, but within six weeks he had a heart attack. His death was very hard for me. It was at a time when we were having a proper relationship – we finally had mutual respect and understanding for each other. I was also starting to do the things that dad had wanted me to do – like graduating, working and buying my first flat. But then he was taken away from me.'

Despite the heartache she suffered, Saira says she can look back and say that her tragic loss helped shape her. 'It made me the woman I am now,' she says defiantly. 'I realised that life is short. I won't dilly-dally, because tomorrow may never come. And now that I have experienced that grief, I know what the feeling is like. I will be prepared for it. It won't ever be easy, but I'll be prepared for it.'

DO YOU BELIEVE IN THE POWER OF PRAYER?

How many times have we said a little prayer to land that dream job or to ask for a poorly loved one to get better? Whether we're religious or not we all tend to find ourselves calling out to someone somewhere for help and guidance. But do we really believe in the power of prayer?

If you are religious and you have faith, then prayer is important and gives you a chance to communicate with a higher being. Whether or not our prayers are actually answered is beside the point. Just having the belief that someone is listening to us during our dark times can be just enough to keep us going.

And what about life after death? What happens when our earthly bodies switch off? Is there a place called heaven where we will be reunited with the loved ones who passed before us? Or, when we die, do we blink off like a light switch? Or do our spirits get reawakened in other bodies?

Perhaps surprisingly, straight-talking Janet says that she prays and even believes that when we die, it's not the end. 'I went to a Church of England school and was raised as an Anglican, and, fundamentally, I do believe in Christianity,' she says. 'I do my best; I'm not going to be a hypocrite and say I'm a perfect Christian. But Jesus preached forgiveness. I think that prayer is something that helps you through tough times.'

She says that this belief in life after death is 'The one thing that's kept me going,' she says. 'Sometimes in my life, when I've had really bad things happen, when people have died, I like to think they really are in a better place.'

This belief in the afterlife helped Janet when, years ago, the son of one of her partners died of cancer. 'That little boy was adorable, and he struggled so hard with various disabilities,' she remembers. 'He struggled so hard at a special school and then, when he was 11, he got stomach cancer and died really quickly. It was devastating.'

At first, her stepson's death made her believe that there simply couldn't be a God, as who could let such a sad thing happen to a child who had already been through so much? 'When that little boy died I thought that there can't be a God,' she says. 'But then I did come to believe again, and that's what got me through that particular time.'

Janet says she wants to encourage more people to have faith in something so that during their worst moments they feel like they are not alone. 'When I see a balloon floating around a room in a hospital, I personally think it's the air conditioning moving that balloon around, nothing more,' she says. 'But if it gives a woman following the death of a child a little bit of comfort to believe otherwise, then fair enough. But a human spirit isn't inside a balloon or in a rainbow or whatever. I believe the spirit goes somewhere else and there is another world.'

Janet says that she is almost embarrassed to speak about her beliefs as she likes to keep them to herself. However, in her mind's eye, she thinks her mother is in another place, 'Sitting on a park bench, smoking a very strong cigarette, along with my sister – because that's my image of them because they smoked their entire life!'

Unsurprisingly, Gloria says that prayer has been very helpful in her life, especially during the tough years her daughter was struggling. 'I do have a very strong faith,' she says. 'It's not to say that I go to church every Sunday. I don't. But it's very important to me. After Caron died, people would ask me afterwards about whether or not I lost my faith because she lost her battle. And I always say no, because I prayed so much when Caron was ill and she actually lived on for seven years as opposed to the prognosis of a year and a half.

I feel that faith is very important to me and I wanted to keep it. And I also never allowed myself to get angry because I just think the angry route is futile.'

LOOSE LESSONS

- Dealing with loss is hard, but life will eventually get better day by day. Take it slowly.

- Losing someone can make you re-evaluate your future – it will highlight what is most important to you.

- If you're feeling like you can't cope, talk to someone. Talking honestly can be a healing process.

GETTING OLDER

ARE YOU SCARED OF AGEING?

Getting older is a shock. When we're 20 years old, 30 can sound a million miles away, while 50... But as we get older time seems to accelerate and the days whiz by so quickly. We can't turn back time, but sometimes with a positive mindset, healthy eating and regular exercise we can try to carry on enjoying life and doing everything we want to do into our old age.

Take Janet, a woman in her seventies who looks almost half her age. She knows there's no going back so she makes the most of her life. 'Everybody wants to age in as good a way as they can, but to deny the ageing process entirely I'm not really comfortable with,' she says. 'I think that ageing is just part of life and I worry that everybody can't face up to dying; they want to extend life as long as possible.'

Janet tries to keep her mind on the present. 'I decided that I'm not going to worry, because you can't achieve anything by worrying. All you can do is get the appropriate tests and be vigilant, but apart from that... don't give it a moment's thought!'

Coleen has also faced up to ageing and admits her fear of it disappeared when she lost her sister Bernie to cancer. That and the cancer diagnosis of two of her other sisters made her realise there was simply no point in fretting about a future she had no control of. 'Selfishly, you do think of your own life and mortality, but it puts things into perspective too, and in a positive way. I stopped worrying about what will happen in four or five years, and how I'll feel hitting 60. Because, all of a sudden, I realised I might not get there. So now I just live every day for what it is.'

Gloria has a fear of ending up in a care home. 'I don't know why I dread the idea of care homes so much,' she says. 'All of my life I've said to my son Michael, "Don't ever put me in a care home!" but he tells me not to worry. Something I have discovered is that the cost of a good care home is practically the same as somebody who could come in and care for you in your home. If I had to have that kind of help, that is what I would opt for.'

SURVIVING THE MENOPAUSE

The menopause is still something few women really, truly understand. Even Nadia admits that when she first realised she was 'going through the change' – to use an old cliché – she knew little of what to expect.

'The menopause was very bad for me,' Nadia reveals. 'The first symptom was that I got depressed and down – I had no idea what it was, though, because the menopause wasn't really talked about.'

Although Nadia says she noticed physical changes during this time, she says she also experienced emotional changes that made her think she had dementia.

'The menopause is dark, very, very dark,' she recounts. 'I had irrational rages – I got really angry out of nowhere and all of a sudden I'd have these flip-outs. I also experienced memory loss, which then made me really paranoid that I had dementia. Before I knew I had the menopause I thought I was getting that. That was petrifying, and I didn't want to tell anybody.'

And there were other alarming symptoms that left Nadia nervous. 'During this time, I was also bleeding for months and months, round the clock. And I remember ringing the doctor and I said, "I'm bleeding a lot." He asked, "Is it a mug-full a day? Are you filling a mug?" And I said, "It's probably about half a mug," and he said, "That's OK then." But it's petrifying – it was just pouring.'

Because Nadia had gone through such an ordeal, she was keen to talk about the menopause on the show. So when a new editor joined the team she and the other women asked to discuss it more.

'Up until then it just wasn't discussed on television because people found it unsavoury!' she exclaims. 'So this meant that many women, like me, were getting hit by symptoms and not knowing what they were! The thing is, women are living a lot longer, we are empowered, and our age group are people with some money. Women over 50 are an incredibly powerful force. Really, all of this stuff that happens to us should be something that we're talking about and we shouldn't feel ashamed.'

To help deal with her experience, Nadia turned to homeopathy, healthy eating, meditation and exercise.

Jane says her experience wasn't as bad as she thought it would be. 'I always feel guilty for saying it, but I found the menopause a positive experience,' she says. 'I did feel a bit like my stuffing had been taken out of me, but then I went on to HRT and that helped. But, for me, it was such a relief to stop caring what people I don't know think, which in social-media days is a good position to be in. And now I'm happy in what I do, I don't feel this constant need to improve myself, and I've taken real solace in my home life. There are periods of time when I go out socially, and I have reached that age when I feel invisible, but I don't care because I'm not invisible to my husband or my kids or my wider family, so I love just being with the people who matter. The rest of it I can take or leave.'

Kaye says she was lucky. 'I didn't have a hard time, which made me a little unsympathetic to others to start with,' she admits. 'Having lots of friends that age, I do appreciate it is hard for some. I remember there was a certain period of time I can identify when the menopause kicked in for me. I remember I was feeling very anxious. I wouldn't say depressed, but for this period I was feeling very bleak. I think that was linked to a hormonal change. But I came out of it naturally and I don't think it particularly affected me that much.'

Kaye thinks women need to talk more about this experience,

although she can understand why it has remained such a taboo subject for so long, even though every woman goes through it. 'I do wish women had access to more information,' she says. 'It should be the norm for us to go to the doctor and be able to have a chat about it. I remember having dinner with a pal once and she said she wasn't sleeping and was eating for 16. I sat and Googled it and identified it as the menopause. How silly that two women of a certain age should be Googling symptoms about something every woman goes through. That tells you we don't talk about it enough.

'Socially, there has been a reticence because it is not seen as a glamorous time of your life; it's when women become "dried up old prunes". It's madness.'

Gloria was lucky too in that her experience wasn't all that bad either. 'My menopause started at 44, but I was fortunate in that I didn't suffer much at all. So I had no hot flushes. All that really happened is that my periods went away. I took lots of supplements, such as vitamin E, vitamin C and phytosome, all prescribed by my homeopathic doctor. I took vitamins to prevent heart disease and against osteoporosis. I also ate an exceptionally healthy diet – lots of broccoli and leafy vegetables. I did plenty of exercise, making sure I walked lots and went on my exercise bike. In other words I did my best.'

Saira admits that while she never worried about getting older, the menopause took her by surprise and threw her life into turmoil. 'No one ever told me about what to expect from the menopause,' she confesses. 'My mum never mentioned it because she came from a generation that never talked about it. It's a funny thing because you still feel young in the head yet your body is ageing; you never feel old. But then I started getting these hot sweats and it hit me like a ton of bricks and I didn't know what to do. I had dark days when I couldn't get out of bed. I had hot sweats, my libido vanished and I was in a depression.'

Luckily for Saira, one of her fellow Loose Women had the answer for her. 'It was Janet who helped me out,' she reveals 'I told her what was going on and she said go on HRT and assured me I'd feel great. So I went to the doctor and it changed my life.'

Now Saira reckons that with more people being open about this stage of life, women are feeling less isolated and empowered. 'Once upon a time, when you said you were going through the menopause people would make a judgement about you. These days women are no longer seeing the menopause as the end of their lives. And it's true. I am living the best life I have ever lived. I don't feel like I have to prove myself any more, it's so liberating. We are still living our lives in spite of the menopause. It's not slowing us down. In some ways it gives us a new lease of life.'

WOULD YOU TAKE A DEMENTIA TEST?

Watching a loved one slowly lose themselves to dementia is just cruel. And, at present, there is no cure. So if you were offered the chance to take a test to see if you were vulnerable, would you take it?

Coleen, who has a history of dementia in her family, says she is not so sure she would want to find out early. 'Obviously I worry about the disease because I've seen my mother go through it, and it is a really cruel disease for everybody, for the whole family,' she says. 'I've also had the cancer issue in my family, so I've had both of those things that I worry about. Now I do get tested all the time for anything cancer-related, I make sure I'm there for all my check-ups because I know with cancer if you catch it early enough there are cures out there and you can stop it. But with dementia you can't. And so therefore that's the one test I wouldn't do, although I worry about it anyway.'

The fear of developing dementia is always in Coleen's mind. 'I get this panic in me of "Have I got the start of it?" because once my mum was diagnosed, I think she'd had it five-to-seven years already. But we'd put it down to mum being really dippy. And we'd moan, "Why does she keep forgetting that?"'

Saira says that she felt reluctant to take a test because it would begin a countdown to when the disease hits. However, after listening to Coleen she now says, 'Before, I thought, "I don't think I want to take the test because it would worry me and spoil my quality of life,"' she explains. 'But hearing about people who live with it for years and their families later feeling guilty for having thought that they were a bit loopy – I wouldn't want anyone to feel guilty because of that time they argued with me. So for that reason I would take the test.'

Saira also feels that if she was aware that she could develop dementia she could prepare for the future. 'It would make me live my life to the fullest, knowing that I've got a limited amount of time,' she says. 'But knowing that my family were with me on it and it wasn't stressful for them.'

Kaye, however, is clear that she would not want to know what lay ahead for her. 'There are various tests for various diseases like cancer, but I have never gone for any of them and I don't think I ever would,' she explains. 'If it was something I could do something about then I would, but there's no cure. That said, if I had the test and I looked likely to get dementia at least I'd get time to get my affairs in order.'

LOOSE LESSONS

- We all get old, so don't let any worry about what is to come cripple you. Make plans for the future.

- If you are going through the menopause, don't be shy and do talk about it. Women everywhere go through it so we need to normalise speaking up about it.

- Enjoy getting older and the ongoing experiences. Embrace every single new day.

INDEX

ACKNOWLEDGEMENTS

The Publishers would like to thank the following people for their hard work in making this book:

The *Loose Women* panellists for allowing us to publish their stories: Jane Moore, Saira Khan, Coleen Nolan, Janet Street-Porter, Gloria Hunniford, Kaye Adams and Nadia Sawalha. The Production team at ITV whose tireless work and support of the project have made the experience so enjoyable: Sally Shelford, Tom Sage, Nicola Penny, Emma Daly, Emma Barrow, Helen Stuart, Mattie Jameson and Vivek Sharma. Daniel Oskiewicz and Fiona Skinner at ITV for their help with the cover. Christian Guiltenane for his sculpting of the manuscript and for his infectious enthusiasm throughout. Mark Harrison for his superb photography, and Shirley Patton of ITV Studios Global Entertainment for managing the complex process of bringing everyone together.